T0154443

Mike McGrath

Java

7th edition

In easy steps is an imprint of In Easy Steps Limited
16 Hamilton Terrace · Holly Walk · Leamington Spa
Warwickshire · United Kingdom · CV32 4LY
www.ineasysteps.com

Seventh Edition

Copyright © 2021 by In Easy Steps Limited. All rights reserved. No part of this book may be reproduced or transmitted in any form or by any means, electronic or mechanical, including photocopying, recording, or by any information storage or retrieval system, without prior written permission from the publisher.

Notice of Liability
Every effort has been made to ensure that this book contains accurate and current information. However, In Easy Steps Limited and the author shall not be liable for any loss or damage suffered by readers as a result of any information contained herein.

Trademarks
All trademarks are acknowledged as belonging to their respective companies.

In Easy Steps Limited supports The Forest Stewardship Council (FSC), the leading international forest certification organization. All our titles that are printed on Greenpeace approved FSC certified paper carry the FSC logo.

FSC
www.fsc.org
MIX
Paper from
responsible sources
FSC® C020837

Printed and bound in the United Kingdom

ISBN 978-1-84078-873-0

Contents

1 Getting started 7

Introduction 8
Installing the JDK 10
Writing a first Java program 12
Compiling & running programs 14
Creating a variable 16
Recognizing data types 18
Creating constants 20
Adding comments 21
Troubleshooting problems 22
Summary 24

2 Performing operations 25

Doing arithmetic 26
Assigning values 28
Comparing values 30
Assessing logic 32
Examining conditions 34
Setting precedence 36
Escaping literals 38
Working with bits 40
Summary 42

3 Making statements 43

Branching with if 44
Branching alternatives 46
Switching branches 48
Looping for 50
Looping while true 52
Doing do-while loops 54
Breaking out of loops 56
Returning control 58
Summary 60

4 Directing values 61

Casting type values 62
Creating variable arrays 64
Passing an argument 66
Passing multiple arguments 68
Looping through elements 70
Changing element values 72
Adding array dimensions 74
Catching exceptions 76
Summary 78

5 Manipulating data 79

Exploring Java classes 80
Doing mathematics 82
Rounding numbers 84
Generating random numbers 86
Managing strings 88
Comparing strings 90
Searching strings 92
Manipulating characters 94
Summary 96

6 Creating classes 97

Forming multiple methods 98
Understanding program scope 100
Forming multiple classes 102
Extending an existing class 104
Creating an object class 106
Producing an object instance 108
Encapsulating properties 110
Constructing object values 112
Summary 114

7 Importing functions 115

Handling files 116
Reading console input 118
Reading files 120
Writing files 122
Sorting array elements 124
Making array lists 126
Managing dates 128
Formatting numbers 130
Summary 132

8 Building interfaces 133

Creating a window 134
Adding push buttons 136
Adding labels 138
Adding text fields 140
Adding item selectors 142
Adding radio buttons 144
Arranging components 146
Changing appearance 148
Summary 150

9 Recognizing events 151

Listening for events 152
Generating events 153
Handling button events 154
Handling item events 156
Reacting to keyboard events 158
Responding to mouse events 160
Announcing messages 162
Requesting input 164
Summary 166

10 Deploying programs 167

Producing an application 168
Distributing programs 170
Building Java archives 172
Deploying applications 173
Creating Android projects 174
Exploring project files 176
Adding resources & controls 178
Inserting Java code 180
Testing the application 182
Deploying Android apps 184
Summary 186

Index 187

Preface

The creation of this book has provided me, Mike McGrath, a welcome opportunity to update my previous books on Java programming with the latest techniques. All examples I have given in this book demonstrate Java features supported by current compilers on both Windows and Linux operating systems, and the book's screenshots illustrate the actual results produced by compiling and executing the listed code, or by implementing code snippets in the Java shell.

Conventions in this book

In order to clarify the code listed in the steps given in each example, I have adopted certain colorization conventions. Components of the Java language itself are colored blue; programmer-specified names are red; numeric and string values are black; and comments are green, like this:

```
// Store then output a text string value.
String message = "Welcome to Java programming!" ;
System.out.println( message ) ;
```

Additionally, in order to identify each source code file described in the steps, a colored icon and file name appears in the margin alongside the steps, like these:

App.java

App.class

App.jar

App.xml

App.html

App.jnlp

Grabbing the source code

For convenience, I have placed source code files from the examples featured in this book into a single ZIP archive. You can obtain the complete archive by following these easy steps:

1. Browse to **www.ineasysteps.com** then navigate to Free Resources and choose the Downloads section
2. Find Java in easy steps, 7th Edition in the list, then click on the hyperlink entitled All Code Examples to download the archive
3. Now, extract the archive contents to any convenient location on your computer

I sincerely hope you enjoy discovering the programming possibilities of Java and have as much fun with it as I did in writing this book.

Mike McGrath

1 Getting started

Welcome to the exciting world of Java programming. This chapter shows how to create and execute simple Java programs, and demonstrates how to store data within programs.

8 Introduction
10 Installing the JDK
12 Writing a first Java program
14 Compiling & running programs
16 Creating a variable
18 Recognizing data types
20 Creating constants
21 Adding comments
22 Troubleshooting problems
24 Summary

Introduction

This is "Duke" – the friendly mascot of the Java programming language.

The Java™ programming language was first developed in 1990 by an engineer at Sun Microsystems named James Gosling. He was unhappy using the C++ programming language so he created a new language that he named "Oak", after the oak tree that he could see from his office window.

As the popularity of the World Wide Web grew, Sun recognized that Gosling's language could be developed for the internet. Consequently, Sun renamed the language "Java" (simply because that name sounded cool) and made it freely available in 1995. Developers around the world quickly adopted this exciting new language and, because of its modular design, were able to create new features that could be added to the core language. The most endearing additional features were retained in subsequent releases of Java as it developed into the comprehensive version of today.

The essence of Java is a library of files called "classes", which each contain small pieces of ready-made proven code. Any of these classes can be incorporated into a new program, like bricks in a wall, so that only a relatively small amount of new code ever needs to be written to complete the program. This saves the programmer a vast amount of time, and largely explains the huge popularity of Java programming. Additionally, this modular arrangement makes it easier to identify any errors than in a single large program.

There is no truth in the rumor that JAVA stands for "Just Another Vague Acronym".

Java technology is both a programming language and a platform. In Java programming, the source code is first written as human-readable plain text files ending with the **.java** extension. These are compiled into machine-readable **.class** files by the **javac** compiler. The **java** interpreter can then execute the program with an instance of the Java Virtual Machine (Java VM):

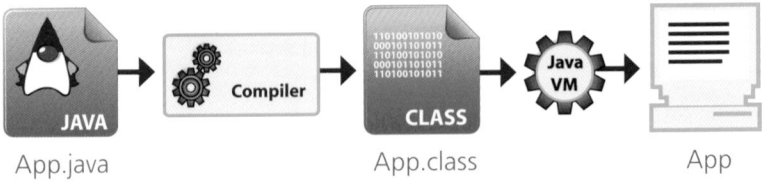

As the Java VM is available on many different operating systems, the same **.class** files are capable of running on Windows, Linux, and Mac operating systems – so Java programmers theoretically enjoy the cross-platform ability to "write once, run anywhere".

In order to create Java programs, the Java class libraries and the **javac** compiler need to be installed on your computer. In order to run Java programs, the **J**ava™ **R**untime **E**nvironment (JRE) needs to be installed to supply the **java** interpreter. All of these components are contained in a freely available package called the **J**ava SE (Standard Edition) **D**evelopment **K**it (JDK).

Discover more about Oracle Java software at **www.oracle.com/java**

The JDK package is available in versions for 32-bit and 64-bit variants of the Linux, Mac, and Windows platforms – select the version for your computer to get started with Java programming.

Oracle JDK

The Oracle Corporation bought the Sun JDK and renamed it to Oracle JDK. This is the formal proprietary version of the Java SE (Standard Edition), maintained by the Oracle team.

OpenJDK

The official reference implementation of the Java SE (Standard Edition) is named "OpenJDK" (Open Java Development Kit). This is a totally free open-source version, supported by Oracle and the Java community at large.

OpenJDK delivers new releases every six months, and several implementations of these are available. The implementation recommended by this book is that provided by the AdoptOpenJDK community group at **adoptopenjdk.net**

Learn more on OpenJDK at **openjdk.java.net**

At the time of writing AdoptOpenJDK is scheduled to soon become EclipseAdoptium, with Java download at **https://projects.eclipse.org/projects/adoptium/downloads**

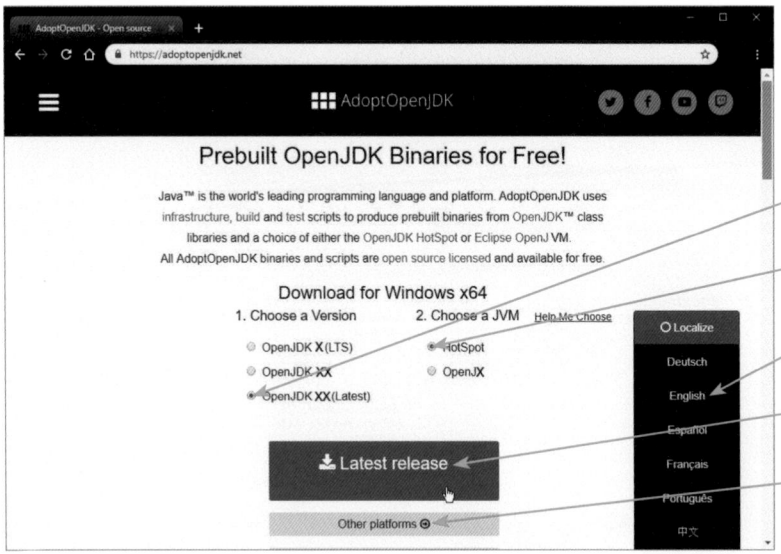

Choose the latest version.

Choose the HotSpot JVM.

Choose your language.

Download your choice.

Or select "Other platforms" and choose the version for your PC.

Installing the JDK

Download the appropriate JDK package for your system from the AdoptOpenJDK website, shown on page 9, then follow these steps to install the Java Development Kit on your computer:

1. Uninstall any previous versions of the JDK and/or Java Runtime Environment (JRE) from your system

2. For Windows, the download is currently a Microsoft Installer (**.msi**) file that will install the JDK package. Click on the download file icon to launch the installer

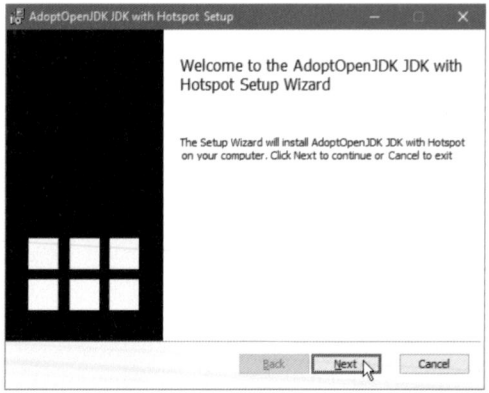

3. Click **Next** to continue, then accept the License Agreement terms and click **Next** once more

4. Change the Location to **C:\Java** and select the "Add to PATH" option, then click **Next** to install the JDK

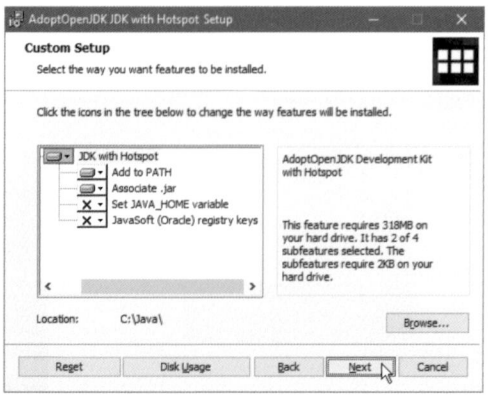

A previous version of the JRE may be installed so your web browser can run Java applets. It is best to uninstall this to avoid confusion with the newer version in the latest JDK.

On Linux, first extract the contents of the download **tar.gz** file to **/usr/Java**. Then add the location of Java's **bin** sub-directory to the system path by editing the **.bashrc** file in your home directory with **PATH=$PATH:/usr/Java/bin** and save the file.

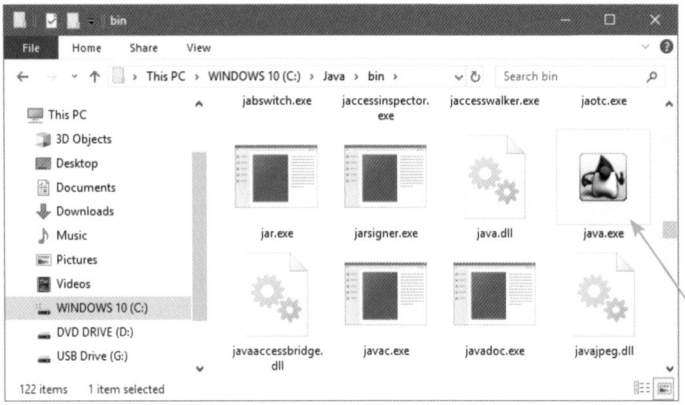

The JDK contains several folders. The **bin** folder holds binary executable files that are the Java compiler (**javac.exe**), Java shell (**jshell.exe**), and the Java VM (**java.exe**).

You are now able to test your Java development environment:

1. Press **Winkey** + **R**, to open a "Run" window, then enter **cmd** to launch a Command Prompt window – or launch a Terminal window on Linux

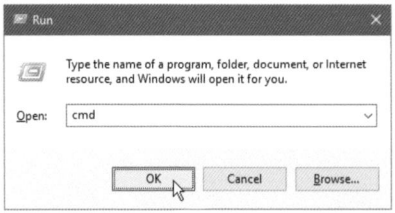

Windows key (Winkey)

2. At the prompt, enter the command **java -version** to see the JDK version number (in place of the Xs shown below)

3. Now, enter a **jshell -version** command to see the Java shell version – and you're ready to begin Java programming!

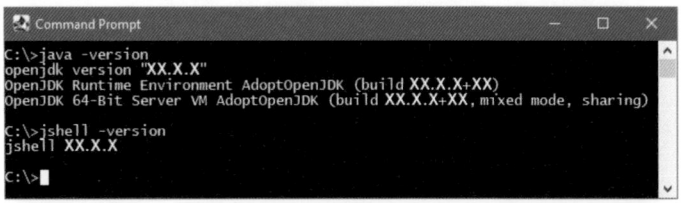

The Java shell **jshell** is an interactive tool that lets you quickly test snippets of code, without the need to first compile the code. It is used in Chapter 2 to demonstrate the various "operators" available in Java programming.

Writing a first Java program

All Java programs start as text files that are later used to create "class" files, which are the actual runnable programs. This means that Java programs can be written in any plain text editor such as the Windows Notepad app or the Nano app on Linux.

Follow these steps to create a simple Java program that will output the traditional first program greeting:

Hello.java

1. Open a plain text editor, like Notepad, and type this code exactly as it is listed – to create a class named "Hello"

```
class Hello
{

}
```

2. Between the curly brackets of the **Hello** class, insert this code – to create a "main" method for the **Hello** class

```
public static void main ( String[] args )
{

}
```

3. Between the curly brackets of the **main** method, insert this line of code – stating what the program will do

```
System.out.println( "Hello World!" ) ;
```

4. Save the file at any convenient location, but be sure to name it precisely as **Hello.java** – the complete program should now look like this:

Java is a case-sensitive language where "Hello" and "hello" are distinctly different – traditionally, Java program names should always begin with an uppercase letter.

Java programs are always saved as their exact program name followed by the ".java" extension.

Hello.java - Notepad

File Edit Format View Help

```
class Hello
{
    public static void main ( String[] args )
    {
        System.out.println( "Hello World!" ) ;
    }
}
```

The separate parts of the program code on the opposite page can be examined individually to understand each part more clearly:

The program container

```
class Hello {     }
```

The program name is declared following the **class** keyword, and followed by a pair of curly brackets. All of the program code that defines the **Hello** class will be contained within these curly brackets.

The main method

```
public static void main ( String[] args ) {          }
```

This fearsome-looking line is the standard code that is used to define the starting point of nearly all Java programs. It will be used in most examples throughout this book exactly as it appears above – so it may be useful to memorize it.

The code declares a method named "main" that will contain the actual program instructions within its curly brackets.

Keywords **public static void** precede the method name to define how the method may be used, and are explained in detail later.

The code **(String[] args)** is useful when passing values to the method, and is also fully explained later in this book.

The statement

```
System.out.println( "Hello World!" ) ;
```

Statements are actual instructions to perform program tasks, and must always end with a semicolon. A method may contain many statements inside its curly brackets to form a "statement block" defining a series of tasks to perform, but here a single statement instructs the program to output a line of text.

Turn to page 14 to discover how to compile and run this program.

All stand-alone Java programs must have a main method.

Create a "MyJava" directory in which to save all your Java program files.

Compiling & running programs

Before a Java program can run, it must first be compiled into a **class** file by the Java compiler. This is located in Java's **bin** sub-directory, and is an application named **javac**. The **bin** sub-directory was added to the system path during installation so that **javac** can be invoked from any system location.

Hot tip

On Windows use the Command Prompt app or Windows PowerShell app to provide a command-line prompt, and on Linux use a Terminal window.

Follow these steps to compile the program on page 13:

1. Open a command-line window, then navigate to the directory where you saved the **Hello.java** source code file

2. Type **javac** followed by a space then the full name of the source code file **Hello.java** and hit the **Enter** key

Hot tip

At a prompt type **javac** and hit Enter to reveal the Java compiler options.

If the **javac** compiler discovers errors in the code it will halt and display a helpful report indicating the nature of the error – see page 22 for troubleshooting problems.

If the **javac** compiler does not find any errors it will create a new file with the program name and the **.class** file extension.

Hot tip

You can also compile the source code from another location if you state the file's full path address to the javac compiler – in this case, **C:\MyJava\Hello.java**

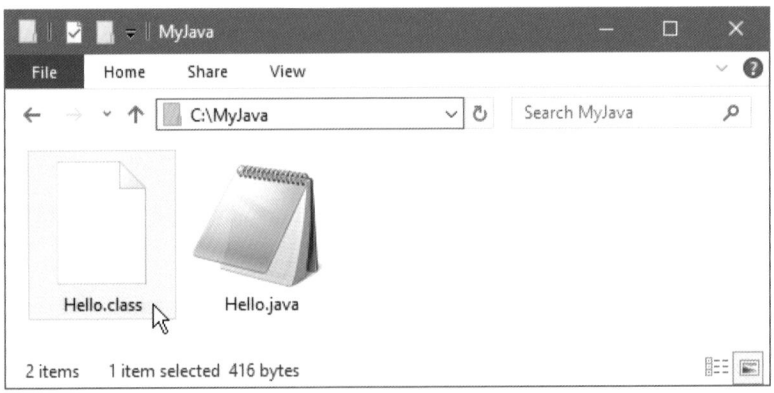

When the Java compiler completes compilation, the command-line prompt window focus returns to the prompt without any confirmation message – and the program is ready to run.

The Java program interpreter is an application named **java** that is located in Java's **bin** sub-directory – alongside the **javac** compiler. As this directory was previously added to the system path during installation the **java** interpreter can be invoked from any location.

Follow these steps to run the program that was compiled using the procedure described on the page opposite:

1. Open a command-line prompt window, then navigate to the directory where the **Hello.class** program file is located

2. At the prompt, type **java** followed by a space then the program name **Hello** and hit the **Enter** key

```
Command Prompt
C:\>cd MyJava

C:\MyJava> java Hello
Hello World!

C:\MyJava>
```

Do not include the .class extension when running a program – only use the program name.

The **Hello** program runs and executes the task defined in the statement within its main method – to output "Hello World!". Upon completion, focus returns to the prompt once more.

The process of compiling and running a Java program is typically combined in sequential steps, and is the same regardless of platform. The screenshot below illustrates the **Hello** program being compiled and run in combined steps on a Linux system:

```
Terminal
File  Edit  View  Search  Terminal  Help
mike ▸ cd MyJava
mike ▸ javac Hello.java
mike ▸ java Hello
Hello World!
mike ▸
```

Creating a variable

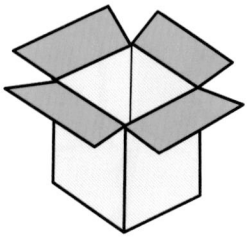

In Java programming, a "variable" is simply a useful container in which a value may be stored for subsequent use by the program. The stored value may be changed (vary) as the program executes its instructions – hence the term "variable".

A variable is created by writing a variable "declaration" in the program, specifying the type of data that variable may contain and a given name for that variable. For example, the **String** data type can be specified to allow a variable named "message" to contain regular text with this declaration:

```
String message ;
```

Variable names are chosen by the programmer but must adhere to certain naming conventions. The variable name may only begin with a letter, dollar sign $, or the underscore character _ , and may subsequently have only letters, digits, dollar signs, or underscore characters. Names are case-sensitive, so "var" and "Var" are distinctly different names, and spaces are not allowed in names.

Variable names should also avoid the Java keywords listed in the table below, as these have special meaning in the Java language.

Each variable declaration must be terminated with a semicolon character – like all other statements.

Strictly speaking, some words in this table are not actually keywords – **true**, **false**, and **null** are all literals; **String** is a special class name; **const** and **goto** are reserved words (currently unused). These are included in the table because they must also be avoided when naming variables.

abstract	default	goto	package	synchronized
assert	do	if	private	this
boolean	double	implements	protected	throw
break	else	import	public	throws
byte	enum	instanceof	return	transient
case	extends	int	short	true
catch	false	interface	static	try
char	final	long	strictfp	void
class	finally	native	String	volatile
const	float	new	super	while
continue	for	null	switch	

As good practice, variables should be named with words or easily recognizable abbreviations, describing that variable's purpose. For example, "button1" or "btn1" to describe button number one. Lowercase letters are preferred for single-word names, such as "gear", and names that consist of multiple words should capitalize the first letter of each subsequent word, such as "gearRatio" – the so-called "camelCase" naming convention.

Once a variable has been declared, it may be assigned an initial value of the appropriate data type using the equals sign = , either in the declaration or later on in the program, then its value can be referenced at any time using the variable's name.

Follow these steps to create a program that declares a variable, which gets initialized in its declaration then changed later:

1. Start a new program named "FirstVariable", containing the standard main method

```
class FirstVariable
{
        public static void main ( String[] args ) {          }
}
```

FirstVariable.java

2. Between the curly brackets of the main method, insert this code to create, initialize, and output a variable

```
String message = "Initial value" ;
System.out.println( message ) ;
```

3. Add these lines to modify and output the variable value

```
message = "Modified value" ;
System.out.println( message ) ;
```

4. Save the program as **FirstVariable.java**, then compile and run the program

If you encounter problems compiling or running the program, you can get help with troubleshooting problems on page 22.

```
Command Prompt
C:\MyJava> javac FirstVariable.java

C:\MyJava> java FirstVariable
Initial value
Modified value

C:\MyJava>
```

Recognizing data types

The most frequently-used data types in Java variable declarations are listed in this table, along with a brief description:

Data type:	Description:	Example:
char	A single Unicode character	'a'
String	Any number of Unicode characters	"my String"
int	An integer number, from -2.14 billion to +2.14 billion	1000
float	A floating-point number, with a decimal point	3.14159265f
boolean	A logical value of either true or false	true

Due to the irregularities of floating-point arithmetic, the **float** data type should never be used for precise values such as currency – see page 130 for details.

Notice that **char** data values must always be surrounded by single quotes, and **String** data values must always be surrounded by double quotes. Also, remember that **float** data values must always have an "f" suffix to ensure they are treated as a **float** value.

In addition to the more common data types above, Java provides these specialized data types for use in exacting circumstances:

Data type:	Description:
byte	Integer number from -128 to +127
short	Integer number from -32,768 to +32,767
long	Positive or negative integer exceeding 2.14 billion
double	Extremely long floating-point number

All data type keywords begin with a lowercase letter except **String** – which is a special class.

Specialized data types are useful in advanced Java programs – the examples in this book mostly use the common data types described in the top table.

Follow these steps to create a Java program that creates, initializes, and outputs variables of all five common data types:

1. Start a new program named "DataTypes" containing the standard main method

```
class DataTypes
{
        public static void main ( String[] args ) {          }
}
```

DataTypes.java

2. Between the curly brackets of the main method, insert these declarations to create and initialize five variables

```
char letter = 'M' ;
String title = "Java in easy steps" ;
int number = 365 ;
float decimal = 98.6f ;
boolean result = true ;
```

Notice how the + character is used here to join (concatenate) text strings and stored variable values.

3. Add these lines to output an appropriate text **String** concatenated to the value of each variable

```
System.out.println( "Initial is " + letter ) ;
System.out.println( "Book is " + title ) ;
System.out.println( "Days are " + number ) ;
System.out.println( "Temperature is " + decimal ) ;
System.out.println( "Answer is " + result ) ;
```

4. Save the program as **DataTypes.java**, then compile and run the program

```
C:\MyJava> javac DataTypes.java

C:\MyJava> java DataTypes
Initial is M
Book is Java in easy steps
Days are 365
Temperature is 98.6
Answer is true

C:\MyJava>
```

The Java compiler will report an error if the program attempts to assign a value of the wrong data type to a variable – try changing the values in this example, then attempt to recompile the program to see the effect.

Creating constants

1000000

The "final" keyword is a modifier that can be used when declaring variables to prevent any subsequent changes to the values that are initially assigned to them. This is useful when storing a fixed value in a program to avoid it becoming altered accidentally.

Variables created to store fixed values in this way are known as "constants", and it is convention to name constants with all uppercase characters – to distinguish them from regular variables. Programs that attempt to change a constant value will not compile, and the **javac** compiler will generate an error message.

Follow these steps to create a Java program featuring constants:

Constants.java

1. Start a new program named "Constants" containing the standard main method

```
class Constants
{
        public static void main ( String[] args ) {          }
}
```

2. Between the curly brackets of the main method, insert this code to create and initialize three integer constants

```
final int TOUCHDOWN = 6 ;
final int CONVERSION = 1 ;
final int FIELDGOAL = 3 ;
```

3. Now, declare four regular integer variables

```
int td , pat , fg , total ;
```

4. Initialize the regular variables – using multiples of the constant values

```
td = 4 * TOUCHDOWN ;
pat = 3 * CONVERSION ;
fg = 2 * FIELDGOAL ;
total = ( td + pat + fg ) ;
```

5. Add this line to display the total score

```
System.out.println( "Score: " + total ) ;
```

6. Save the program as **Constants.java**, then compile and run the program to see the output, Score: 33
(4 x 6 = 24, 3 x 1 = 3, 2 x 3 = 6, so 24 + 3 + 6 = 33).

The * asterisk character is used here to multiply the constant values, and parentheses surround their addition for clarity.

Adding comments

When programming in any language, it is good practice to add comments to program code to explain each particular section. This makes the code more easily understood by others, and by yourself when revisiting a piece of code after a period of absence.

In Java programming, comments can be added across multiple lines between /* and */ comment identifiers, or on a single line after a // comment identifier. Anything appearing between /* and */, or on a line after //, is completely ignored by the **javac** compiler.

When comments have been added to the **Constants.java** program, described opposite, the source code might look like this:

```
/*
        A program to demonstrate constant variables.
*/

class Constants
{
        public static void main( String args[] )
        {
                // Constant score values.
                final int TOUCHDOWN = 6 ;
                final int CONVERSION = 1 ;
                final int FIELDGOAL = 3 ;

                // Calculate points scored.
                int td , pat , fg , total ;
                td = 4 * TOUCHDOWN ;            // 4x6=24
                pat = 3 * CONVERSION ;          // 3x1= 3
                fg  = 2 * FIELDGOAL ;           // 2x3= 6
                total = ( td + pat + fg ) ;     // 24+3+6=33

                // Output calculated total.
                System.out.println( "Score: " + total ) ;
        }
}
```

Constants.java (commented)

You can add a statement that attempts to change the value of a constant, then try to recompile the program to see the resulting error message.

Saved with comments, the program compiles and runs as normal:

```
Command Prompt

C:\MyJava> javac Constants.java

C:\MyJava> java Constants
Score: 33

C:\MyJava>
```

Troubleshooting problems

Sometimes, the **javac** compiler or **java** interpreter will complain about errors, so it's useful to understand their cause and how to quickly resolve the problem. In order to demonstrate some common error reports, this code contains some deliberate errors:

Test.java

```
class test
{
        public static void main ( String[] args )
        {
                String text ;
                System.out.println( "Test " + text )
        }
}
```

A first attempt to compile **Test.java** throws up this error report:

```
Command Prompt
C:\MyJava> javac Test.java
'javac' is not recognized as an internal or external command,
operable program or batch file.

C:\MyJava>
```

- Cause – the **javac** compiler cannot be found.
- Solution – edit your system environment with the command
  setx path "%path%;C:\Java\bin"
  or use the full path to invoke the compiler with the command
  C:\Java\bin\javac Test.java

```
Command Prompt
C:\MyJava> javac Test.java
error: file not found: Test.java
Usage: javac <options> <source files>
use --help for a list of possible options

C:\MyJava>
```

- Cause – the file **Test.java** cannot be found.
- Solution – navigate to the directory where the file is located, or use the full path address to the file in the command.

To edit the environment variables in Windows, you can open the **System Properties**, **Advanced** tab and click the **Environment Variables** button. Select **Path**, **Edit** and add **C:\Java\bin**, then click **OK** to apply the change.

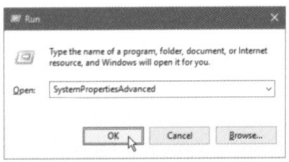

```
Command Prompt
C:\MyJava>  javac Test.java
Test.java:6: error: ';' expected
                System.out.println( "Test " + text )
                                                    ^
1 error
```

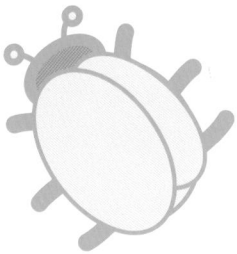

- Cause – the statement is not terminated correctly.
- Solution – in the source code add a semicolon at the end of the statement, then save the file to apply the change.

```
Command Prompt
C:\MyJava>  javac Test.java
Test.java:1: error: class test is public, should be declared in a
 file named test.java
public class test
       ^
1 error
```

- Cause – the program name and class name do not match.
- Solution – in the source code change the class name from **test** to **Test**, then save the file to apply the change.

```
Command Prompt
C:\MyJava>  javac Test.java
Test.java:6: error: variable text might not have been initialized

                System.out.println( "Test " + text ) ;
                                                    ^
1 error
```

- Cause – the variable **text** has no value.
- Solution – in the variable declaration assign the variable a valid **String** value (for instance **= "success"**) then save the file.

```
Command Prompt
C:\MyJava>  javac Test.java

C:\MyJava> java Test
Test success

C:\MyJava>
```

You must run the program from within its directory – you cannot use a path address, as the Java launcher requires a program name, not a file name.

Summary

- Java is both a programming language and a runtime platform.
- Java programs are written as plain text files with a **.java** file extension.
- The Java compiler **javac** creates compiled **.class** program files from original **.java** source code files.
- The Java interpreter **java** executes compiled programs using an instance of the Java Virtual Machine.
- The Java VM is available on many operating system platforms.
- Adding Java's **bin** sub-directory to the system **PATH** variable allows the **javac** compiler to be invoked from anywhere.
- Java is a case-sensitive language.
- The standard **main** method is the entry point for Java programs.
- The **System.out.println()** statement outputs text.
- A Java program file name must exactly match its class name.
- Java variables can only be named in accordance with specified naming conventions, and must avoid the Java keywords.
- In Java programming, each statement must be terminated by a semicolon character.
- The most common Java data types are **String**, **int**, **char**, **float** and **boolean**.
- **String** values must be enclosed in double quotes; **char** values in single quotes; and **float** values must have an "f" suffix.
- The **final** keyword can be used to create a constant variable.
- Comments can be added to Java source code between /* and */, on one or more lines, or after // on a single line.
- Error reports identify compiler and runtime problems.

2 Performing operations

This chapter demonstrates the various operators that are used to create expressions in Java programs.

26 Doing arithmetic

28 Assigning values

30 Comparing values

32 Assessing logic

34 Examining conditions

36 Setting precedence

38 Escaping literals

40 Working with bits

42 Summary

Doing arithmetic

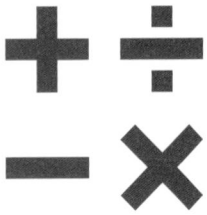

Arithmetical operators, listed in the table below, are used to create expressions in Java programs that return a single resulting value. For example, the expression **4 * 2** returns the value **8**.

Operator:	Operation:
+	Addition (and concatenates **String** values)
-	Subtraction
*	Multiplication
/	Division
%	Modulus
++	Increment
--	Decrement

Division of **int** values will truncate any fractional part. For example, 11/4 = 2, whereas division of **float** values 11/4 = 2.75.

The increment operator **++** and decrement operator **--** return the result of modifying a single given operand by a value of one. For example, **4++** returns the value **5**, and **4--** returns the value **3**.

All other arithmetic operators return the result of an operation performed on two given operands, and act as you would expect. For example, the expression **5 + 2** returns **7**.

Increment and decrement operators are typically used to count the iterations in the **for** loop constructs, introduced on page 50.

The modulus operator divides the first operand by the second operand and returns the remainder of the operation. For example, **32 % 5** returns **2** – five divides into 32 six times, with 2 remainder.

The operation performed by the addition operator + depends on the type of its given operands. Where both operands are numeric values it will return the total sum value of those numbers, but where the operands are **String** values it will return a single concatenated **String** – combining the text in each **String** operand. For example, **"Java "** + **"Arithmetic"** returns **"Java Arithmetic"**.

Follow these steps to explore the Java arithmetic operators in the Java shell:

1. Open a command-line prompt window, then type **jshell** and hit the **Enter** key to launch the Java shell

2. Next, enter statements to initialize three variables
int num = 100 ; int factor = 20 ; int sum = 0 ;

```
Command Prompt - jshell
C:\MyJava> jshell
|  Welcome to JShell
|  For an introduction type: /help intro

jshell> int num = 100 ; int factor = 20 ; int sum = 0 ;
num ==> 100
factor ==> 20
sum ==> 0

jshell>
```

3. Next, separately enter statements to perform addition and subtraction operations, displaying each result
sum = num + factor ;
sum = num - factor ;

```
Command Prompt - jshell
jshell> sum = num + factor ;
sum ==> 120

jshell> sum = num - factor ;
sum ==> 80
```

4. Now, separately enter statements to perform multiplication and division operations, displaying each result
sum = num * factor ;
sum = num / factor ;

```
Command Prompt - jshell
jshell> sum = num * factor ;
sum ==> 2000

jshell> sum = num / factor ;
sum ==> 5
```

Java must be installed on your system path to launch the Java shell from any prompt – see Installing on page 10 and Troubleshooting on page 22 for details.

Optionally, the semicolon character may be omitted at the end of single statements entered into the shell, but these are required when writing Java programs for compilation. Semicolons are included in the shell examples in this chapter to aid code consistency.

Assigning values

Assignment operators, listed in the table below, are used to assign the result of an expression. All except the simple = operator are the shorthand form of a longer equivalent expression:

Operator:	Example:	Equivalent:
=	a = b	a = b
+=	a += b	a = a + b
-=	a -= b	a = a - b
*=	a *= b	a = a * b
/=	a /= b	a = a / b
%=	a %= b	a = a % b

It is important to regard the = operator to mean "assign", rather than "equals", to avoid confusion with the == equality operator.

In the example **a = b**, the value stored in the variable named **b** is assigned to the variable named **a**, so that value becomes the new value stored in **a** – replacing any value it previously contained.

The += operator is useful to add a value onto an existing value stored in a variable – keeping a "running total".

The example **a += b** first calculates the sum total of the values stored in the variables named **a** and **b**, then assigns the resulting total to variable **a**. A program might then contain a further assignment **a += c** that calculates the total stored in variables named **a** and **c**, then assigns that new total to variable **a** – adding the value of **c** to the value it previously contained.

All the other assignment operators work in the same way by first performing the arithmetical calculation on the two stored values, then assigning the result to the first variable – to become its new stored value.

The == equality operator compares values, and is fully explained on page 30.

Follow these steps to explore the Java assignment operators in the Java shell:

1. Open a command-line prompt window, then type **jshell** and hit the **Enter** key to launch the Java shell

2. Next, enter statements to initialize two **String** variables
String txt = "Super " ; String lang = "Java" ;

3. Now, separately enter statements to add and assign a **String** value, then display the concatenated string result
txt += lang ; txt ;

```
Command Prompt - jshell

C:\MyJava> jshell

jshell> String txt = "Super " ; String lang = "Java" ;
txt ==> "Super "
lang ==> "Java"

jshell> txt += lang ;
$3 ==> "Super Java"

jshell> txt ;
txt ==> "Super Java"

jshell>
```

4. Then, enter statements to initialize two integer variables
int sum = 10 ; int num = 20 ;

5. Separately enter statements to add and assign an **int** value, then display the totaled integer result
sum += num ; sum ;

```
Command Prompt - jshell

jshell> int sum = 10 ; int num = 20 ;
sum ==> 10
num ==> 20

jshell> sum += num ;
$7 ==> 30

jshell> sum ;
sum ==> 30
```

The Java shell creates internal **$**-prefixed numbered variables containing the result of an evaluation. Here, internal variables **$3** and **$7** contain evaluation results.

Assignment of the wrong data type to a variable will cause an error.

Comparing values

Comparison operators, listed in the table below, are used to compare two values in an expression and return a single Boolean value of **true** or **false** – describing the result of that comparison.

Operator:	Comparison:
==	Equality
!=	Inequality
>	Greater than
>=	Greater than, or equal to
<	Less than
<=	Less than, or equal to

The == equality operator compares two operands, and will return **true** if both are exactly equal in value. If both are the same number they are equal, or if both are **String** values containing the same characters in the same order they are equal. Boolean operands that are both **true**, or that are both **false**, are equal.

Conversely, the != inequality operator returns **true** if two operands are not equal – applying the same rules as the equality operator.

Equality and inequality operators are useful in testing the state of two variables to perform "conditional branching" of a program – proceeding in different directions according to the condition.

The > "greater than" operator compares two operands, and will return **true** if the first is greater in value than the second.

The < "less than" operator makes the same comparison, but returns true if the first operand is less in value than the second.

Adding the = assignment operator after the > "greater than" operator, or after the < "less than" operator, makes it also return **true** when the two operands are exactly equal in value.

The < less than operator is typically used to test a counter value in a loop – an example of this can be found on page 50.

Follow these steps to explore the Java comparison operators in the Java shell:

1. Open a command-line prompt window, then type **jshell** and hit the **Enter** key to launch the Java shell

2. Next, enter statements to initialize two **String** variables
String txt = "Super " ; String lang = "Java" ;

3. Now, separately enter statements to initialize a **boolean** variable and display the result of **String** value comparisons for equality and inequality
boolean state = (txt == lang) ;
state = (txt != lang) ;

```
Command Prompt - jshell

C:\MyJava> jshell

jshell> String txt = "Super " ; String lang = "Java" ;
txt ==> "Super "
lang ==> "Java"

jshell> boolean state = ( txt == lang ) ;
state ==> false

jshell> state = ( txt != lang ) ;
state ==> true
```

4. In a similar way, separately enter these statements to display the result of **int** value comparisons for greater and lesser numeric value
int dozen = 12 ; int score = 20 ;
state = (dozen > score) ;
state = (dozen < score) ;

```
Command Prompt - jshell

jshell> int dozen = 12 ; int score = 20 ;
dozen ==> 12
score ==> 20

jshell> state = ( dozen > score ) ;
state ==> false

jshell> state = ( dozen < score ) ;
state ==> true
```

You can discover more options within the Java shell by entering the **/help** command.

Here it's untrue (**false**) that the **String** values are equal, but it is **true** that they are unequal.

Notice how an expression can be contained in parentheses for better readability.

Assessing logic

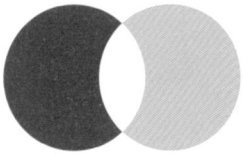

Logical operators, listed in the table below, are used to combine multiple expressions that each return a Boolean value – into a complex expression that returns a single Boolean value.

Operator:	Operation:
&&	Logical AND
||	Logical OR
!	Logical NOT

Logical operators are used with operands that have the Boolean values of **true** or **false**, or values that can convert to **true** or **false**.

The logical **&&** AND operator will evaluate two operands and return **true** only if both operands are themselves **true**. Otherwise, the logical **&&** operator will return **false**. This evaluation can be used in conditional branching, where a program will only perform a certain action when two tested conditions are both true.

Unlike the logical **&&** operator that needs two operands to be **true**, the logical **||** OR operator will evaluate its two operands and return **true** if either one of the operands is **true** – it will only return **false** when neither operand is **true**. This is useful in Java programming to perform a certain action when either one of two test conditions has been met.

The logical **!** NOT operator is a "unary" operator that is used before a single operand. It returns the inverse Boolean value of the given operand – reversing **true** to **false**, and **false** to **true**. It's useful in Java programs to toggle the value of a variable in successive loop iterations with a statement like **goState=!goState**. This ensures that on each pass of the loop the value is changed, like flicking a light switch on and off.

The term "Boolean" refers to a system of logical thought developed by the English mathematician George Boole (1815-1864).

Follow these steps to explore logical operators in the Java shell:

1. Open a command-line prompt window, then type **jshell** and hit the **Enter** key to launch the Java shell

2. Next, enter statements to initialize two **boolean** variables
boolean yes = true ; boolean no = false ;

3. Enter statements to test if both conditions are true
boolean result = (yes && yes) ; result = (yes && no) ;

```
Command Prompt - jshell

C:\MyJava> jshell

jshell> boolean yes = true ; boolean no = false ;
yes ==> true
no ==> false

jshell> boolean result = ( yes && yes ) ;
result ==> true

jshell> result = ( yes && no ) ;
result ==> false
```

4. Enter statements to test if either of the conditions is true
result = (yes || yes) ;
result = (yes || no) ;
result = (no || no) ;

5. Enter statements to show an original and inverse value
result = yes ; result = !yes ;

```
Command Prompt - jshell

jshell> result = ( yes || yes ) ;
result ==> true

jshell> result = ( yes || no ) ;
result ==> true

jshell> result = ( no || no ) ;
result ==> false

jshell> result = yes; result = !yes ;
result ==> true
result ==> false
```

The Java shell is also known as a "REPL" – an acronym for Read, Evaluate, Print, Loop that describes this type of interactive tool.

Notice that **false && false** returns **false**, not **true** – demonstrating the maxim that "two wrongs don't make a right".

The value returned by the ! NOT logical operator is the inverse of the stored value – the stored value itself remains unchanged.

Examining conditions

Possibly the all-time favorite operator of the Java programmer is the **?** : conditional operator that makes a powerful statement very concisely. Its unusual syntax can seem tricky to understand at first, but it is well worth getting to know this useful operator.

The conditional operator first evaluates an expression for a **true** or **false** value, then returns one of two given operands depending on the result of the evaluation. Its syntax looks like this:

(*boolean-expression* **) ?** *if-true-return-this* **:** *if-false-return-this* **;**

Each specified operand alternative allows the program to progress according to the Boolean value returned by the tested expression. For instance, the alternatives might return a **String** value:

status = (quit == true) ? "Done!" : "Continuing..." ;

In this case, when the **quit** variable is **true** the conditional operator assigns the value of its first operand to the **status** variable; otherwise, it assigns its second operand value instead.

A shorthand available when coding Java programs allows expressions to optionally omit **== true** when evaluating a simple Boolean value, so the example above can be written simply as:

status = (quit) ? "Done!" : "Continuing..." ;

The conditional operator can return values of any data type and employ any valid test expression. For instance, the expression might use the greater than **>** operator to evaluate two numeric values then return a Boolean value depending on the result:

busted = (speed > speedLimit) ? true : false ;

Similarly, the conditional operator might employ the inequality **!=** operator to evaluate a **String** value then return a numeric value depending on the result:

bodyTemperature = (scale != "Celsius") ? 98.6 : 37.0 ;

The conditional operator is also known as the "ternary" operator.

Follow these steps to explore the Java conditional operator in the Java shell:

1. Open a command-line prompt window, then type **jshell** and hit the **Enter** key to launch the Java shell

2. Next, enter statements to initialize two **int** variables
int num1 = 1357 ; int num2 = 2468 ;

3. Declare a further variable to store a test result **String**
String result ;

4. Enter this statement to determine whether the first integer value is an odd or even number
result = (num1 % 2 != 0) ? "Odd" : "Even" ;

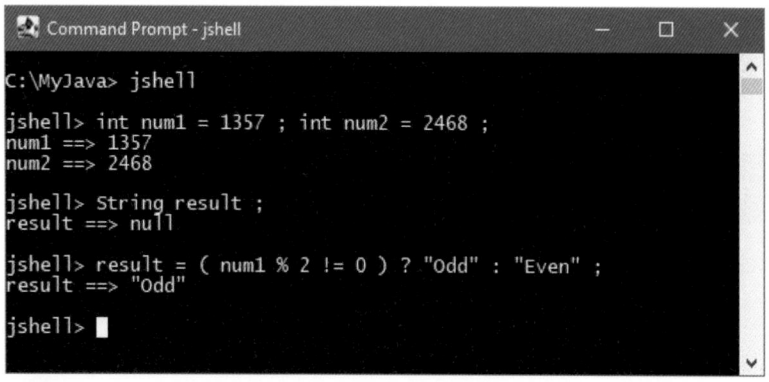

5. Now, enter this statement to determine whether the second integer value is an odd or even number
result = (num2 % 2 != 0) ? "Odd" : "Even" ;

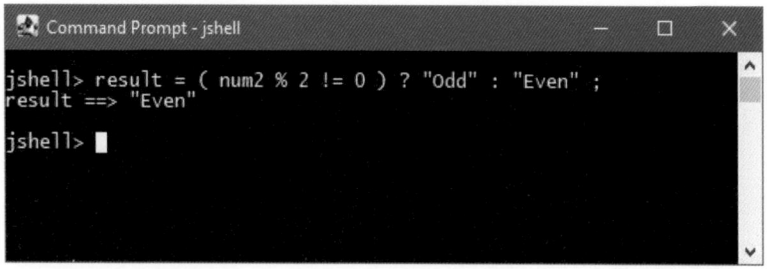

You can also start the Java shell with the command **jshell --feedback verbose** to receive descriptive output after each evaluation.

Notice that an uninitialized **String** variable returns a special **null** value – indicating that it contains nothing whatsoever.

Here, the expression evaluates as true when there is any remainder.

Setting precedence

Complex expressions, which contain multiple operators and operands, can be ambiguous unless the order in which the operations should be executed is clear. This lack of clarity can easily cause different results to be implied by the same expression. For example, consider this complex expression:

num = 8 + 4 * 2 ;

Working left to right: **8 + 4 = 12**, and **12 * 2 = 24**, so **num = 24**. But working right to left: **2 * 4 = 8**, and **8 + 8 = 16**, so **num = 16**.

The Java programmer can explicitly specify which operation should be executed first by adding parentheses to signify which operator has precedence. In this case, **(8 + 4) * 2** ensures that the addition is performed before the multiplication – so the result is 24, not 16. Conversely, **8 + (4 * 2)** performs the multiplication first – so the result is 16, not 24.

Where parentheses do not explicitly specify operator precedence Java follows the default precedence order listed in the table below, from first at the top to last at the bottom:

Operator:	Description:
++ -- !	Increment, Decrement, Logical NOT
* / %	Multiplication, Division, Modulus
+ -	Addition, Subtraction
> >= < <=	Greater than, Greater than or equal to Less than, Less than or equal to
== !=	Equality, Inequality
&&	Logical AND
||	Logical OR
? :	Conditional
= += -= *= /= %=	Assignment

Operators of equal precedence are handled in the order they appear in the expression – from left to right.

Follow these steps to explore operator precedence in the Java shell:

1. Open a command-line prompt window, then type **jshell** and hit the **Enter** key to launch the Java shell

2. Next, enter a statement to display the result of evaluating an expression that uses default operator precedence
int sum = 32 - 8 + 16 * 2 ;

```
Command Prompt - jshell
C:\MyJava> jshell
jshell> int sum = 32 - 8 + 16 * 2 ;
sum ==> 56
jshell>
```

3. Now, enter a statement to display the result of evaluating the same expression – but giving addition and subtraction precedence over multiplication
sum = (32 - 8 + 16) * 2 ;

```
Command Prompt - jshell
jshell> sum = ( 32 - 8 + 16 ) * 2 ;
sum ==> 80
jshell>
```

4. Finally, enter a statement to display the result of evaluating the same expression once more – but now where operation precedence order is first addition, then subtraction, and then multiplication
sum = (32 - (8 + 16)) * 2 ;

```
Command Prompt - jshell
jshell> sum = ( 32 - ( 8 + 16 ) ) * 2 ;
sum ==> 16
jshell>
```

Where expressions have multiple nested parentheses, the innermost takes precedence.

How it works –
Step 2...
16 x 2 = 32, + 24 = 56
Step 3...
24 + 16 = 40, x 2 = 80
Step 4...
32 - 24 = 8, x 2 = 16

This chapter has so far used the Java shell **jshell** to explore the various Java operators by evaluating code snippets. Ensuing examples will use the Java compiler **javac** and Java runtime **java** to create and execute programs. You can quit the Java shell to return to a regular prompt with the command **/exit**.

Escaping literals

The numerical and text values in Java programs are known as "literals" – they represent nothing but are, literally, what you see.

Literals are normally detached from the keywords of the Java language, but where double quotes or single quotes are required within a **String** value it is necessary to indicate that the quote character is to be treated literally to avoid prematurely terminating the **String**. This is easily achieved by immediately prefixing each nested quote character with the \ escape operator. For example, including a quote within a **String** variable, like this:

```
String quote = " \"Fortune favors the brave.\" said Virgil ";
```

Additionally, the \ escape operator offers a variety of useful escape sequences for simple output formatting:

Escape:	Description:
\n	Newline
\t	Tab
\b	Backspace
\r	Carriage return
\f	Formfeed
****	Backslash
\'	Single quote mark
\"	Double quote mark

Single quotes can be nested within double quotes as an alternative to escaping quote characters.

The **\n** newline escape sequence is frequently used within long **String** values to display the output on multiple lines. Similarly, the **\t** tab escape sequence is frequently used to display the output in columns. Using a combination of **\n** newline and **\t** tab escape sequences allows the output to be formatted in both rows and columns – to resemble a table.

Follow these steps to create a Java program using escape sequences to format the output:

1. Start a new program named "Escape" containing the standard main method

```
class Escape
{
        public static void main( String[] args ) {          }
}
```

Escape.java

2. Between the curly brackets of the main method, insert this code to build a **String** containing a formatted table title and column headings

```
String header = "\n\tNEW YORK 3-DAY FORECAST:\n" ;
header += "\n\tDay\t\tHigh\tLow\tConditions\n" ;
header += "\t---\t\t----\t---\t----------\n" ;
```

3. Add these lines to build a **String** containing formatted table cell data

```
String forecast = "\tSunday\t\t68F\t48F\tSunny\n" ;
forecast += "\tMonday\t\t69F\t57F\tSunny\n" ;
forecast += "\tTuesday\t\t71F\t50F\tCloudy\n" ;
```

4. Now, add this line to output both formatted **String** values

```
System.out.print( header + forecast ) ;
```

5. Save the program as **Escape.java**, then compile and run the program

In this case, escape sequences add newlines so the **print()** method is used here – rather than the **println()** method that automatically adds a newline after output.

```
Command Prompt
C:\MyJava> javac Escape.java

C:\MyJava> java Escape

        NEW YORK 3-DAY FORECAST:

        Day             High    Low     Conditions
        ---             ----    ---     ----------
        Sunday          68F     48F     Sunny
        Monday          69F     57F     Sunny
        Tuesday         71F     50F     Cloudy

C:\MyJava>
```

Working with bits

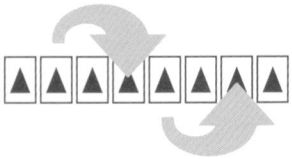

In addition to the regular operators described earlier in this chapter, Java provides special operators for binary arithmetic. These are less commonly used than other operators, but are briefly discussed here to simply provide an awareness of their existence.

The Java "bitwise" operators can be used with the **int** integer data type to manipulate the bits of the binary representation of a value. This requires an understanding of binary numbering, where eight bits in a byte represent decimal values zero to 255. For example, 53 is binary **00110101**
(**0** x 128, **0** x 64, **1** x 32, **1** x 16, **0** x 8, **1** x 4, **0** x 2, **1** x 1).

Binary addition operations are performed like decimal arithmetic:

```
      53   =   00110101
+      7   =   00000111
      60   =   00111100
```

The bitwise operators, listed below, allow more specialized operations to be performed in binary arithmetic.

Operator:	Operation:	Example:	Result:
&	AND	**a & b**	1 if both bits are 1
|	OR	**a | b**	1 if either bit is 1
^	XOR	**a ^ b**	1 if both bits differ
~	NOT	**~a**	Inverts the bits
<<	Left shift	***n* << *p***	Moves *n* bits *p* left
>>	Right shift	***n* >> *p***	Moves *n* bits *p* right

Don't confuse the logical AND operator **&&** with the bitwise **&** operator, or the logical OR operator **||** with the bitwise **|** operator.

For example, using the bitwise **&** operator in binary arithmetic:

```
      53   =   00110101
&      7   =   00000111
       5   =   00000101
```

A common use of bitwise operators combines several values in a single variable for efficiency. For instance, a program with eight "flag" **int** variables, with values of 1 or 0 (representing on and off states), requires 32 bits of memory for each variable – 256 bits in total. These values only really require a single bit, however, so eight flags can be combined in a single **byte** variable – using one bit per flag. The status of each flag can be retrieved with bitwise operations:

Bitwise.java

1. Start a new program named "Bitwise" containing the standard main method

```
class Bitwise
{
        public static void main( String[] args ) {          }
}
```

2. Between the curly brackets of the main method, insert this code to declare and initialize a byte variable with a value representing the total status of up to eight flags

```
byte fs = 53 ;   // Combined flag status of 00110101
```

How it works –
The binary representation of 53 is **00110101** so the set bits are...
1 + 4 + 16 + 32 = 53

3. Add these lines to retrieve the status of each flag

```
System.out.println("Flag 1: "+(( (fs&1)>0) ? "ON" : "off"));
System.out.println("Flag 2: "+(( (fs&2)>0) ? "ON" : "off"));
System.out.println("Flag 3: "+(( (fs&4)>0) ? "ON" : "off"));
System.out.println("Flag 4: "+(( (fs&8)>0) ? "ON" : "off"));
System.out.println("Flag 5: "+(( (fs&16)>0)? "ON" : "off"));
System.out.println("Flag 6: "+(( (fs&32)>0)? "ON" : "off"));
System.out.println("Flag 7: "+(( (fs&64)>0)? "ON" : "off"));
System.out.println("Flag 8: "+(( (fs&128)>0)?"ON": "off"));
```

4. Save the program as **Bitwise.java** then compile and run the program:

```
Command Prompt
C:\MyJava> javac Bitwise.java

C:\MyJava> java Bitwise
Flag 1: ON
Flag 2: off
Flag 3: ON
Flag 4: off
Flag 5: ON
Flag 6: ON
Flag 7: off
Flag 8: off
```

Here, the bitwise **&** operation returns one or zero to determine each flag's status.

Summary

- Arithmetical operators can form expressions with two operands for addition **+**, subtraction **-**, multiplication *****, division **/**, or modulus **%**.
- Increment **++** and decrement **--** operators modify a single operand by a value of one.
- The assignment **=** operator can be combined with an arithmetical operator to perform an arithmetical calculation then assign its result.
- Comparison operators can form expressions comparing two operands for equality **==**, inequality **!=**, greater **>**, or lesser **<** values.
- The assignment **=** operator can be combined with the greater than **>** or lesser than **<** operator to also return **true** when equal.
- Logical **&&** and **||** operators form expressions evaluating two operands to return a Boolean value of either **true** or **false**.
- The logical **!** operator returns the inverse Boolean value of a single operand.
- A conditional **? :** operator evaluates a given Boolean expression and returns one of two operands, depending on its result.
- Expressions evaluating a Boolean expression for a **true** value may optionally omit **== true**.
- It is important to explicitly set operator precedence in complex expressions by adding parentheses **( )**.
- The backslash escape **** operator can be used to prefix quote characters within **String** values to prevent syntax errors.
- Escape sequences **\n** newline and **\t** tab provide simple output formatting.
- Bitwise operators can be useful to perform binary arithmetic in specialized situations.

3 Making statements

This chapter demonstrates the various keywords that are used to create branching in Java programs.

44 Branching with if

46 Branching alternatives

48 Switching branches

50 Looping for

52 Looping while true

54 Doing do-while loops

56 Breaking out of loops

58 Returning control

60 Summary

Branching with if

The **if** keyword performs a conditional test to evaluate an expression for a Boolean value. A statement following the expression will only be executed when the evaluation is **true**, otherwise the program proceeds on to subsequent code – pursuing the next "branch". The **if** statement syntax looks like this:

if (*test-expression*) *code-to-be-executed-when-true* ;

The code to be executed can contain multiple statements if they are enclosed within curly brackets to form a "statement block":

If.java

1. Start a new program named "If" containing the standard main method

```
class If
{
        public static void main ( String[] args) {          }
}
```

2. Between the curly brackets of the main method, insert this simple conditional test that executes a single statement when one number is greater than another

```
if ( 5 > 1 ) System.out.println( "Five is greater than one." ) ;
```

3. Add a second conditional test, which executes an entire statement block when one number is less than another

```
if ( 2 < 4 )
{
        System.out.println( "Two is less than four." ) ;
        System.out.println( "Test succeeded." ) ;
}
```

4. Save the program as **If.java** then compile and run the program to see all statements get executed – because both tests evaluate as **true** in this case:

Expressions can utilize the **true** and **false** keywords. The test expression **(2 < 4)** is shorthand for **(2 < 4 == true)**.

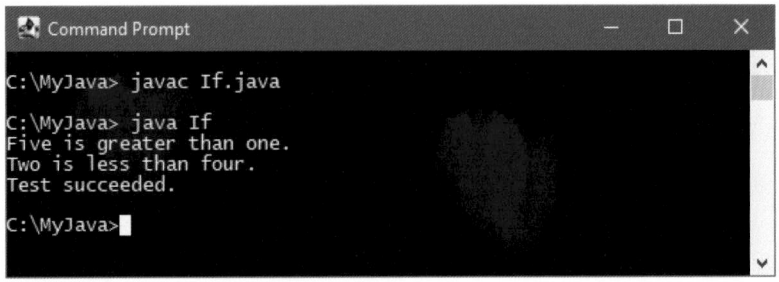

A conditional test can also evaluate a complex expression to test multiple conditions for a Boolean value. Parentheses enclose each test condition to establish precedence – so they get evaluated first. The Boolean **&&** AND operator ensures the complex expression will only return **true** when both tested conditions are true:

if ((*test-condition1*) **&&** (*test-condition2*)) *execute-this-code* ;

The Boolean **||** OR operator ensures a complex expression will only return **true** when either one of the tested conditions is true:

if ((*test-condition1*) **||** (*test-condition2*)) *execute-this-code* ;

A combination of these can form longer complex expressions:

The range can be extended to include the upper and lower limits using the **>=** and **<=** operators.

5. Inside the main method of **If.java** insert this line to declare and initialize an integer variable named **num**
int num = 8 ;

6. Add a third conditional test that executes a statement when the value of the **num** variable is within a specified range, or when it's exactly equal to a specified value
if (((num > 5) && (num < 10)) || (num == 12))
System.out.println("Number is 6-9 inclusive, or 12") ;

7. Recompile the program, and run it once more to see the statement after the complex expression get executed

```
Command Prompt
C:\MyJava> javac If.java

C:\MyJava> java If
Five is greater than one.
Two is less than four.
Test succeeded.
Number is 6-9 inclusive, or 12

C:\MyJava>
```

The complex expression uses the **==** equality operator to specify an exact match, not the **=** assignment operator.

8. Change the value assigned to the **num** variable so it is neither within the specified range 6-9, or exactly 12. Recompile the program, and run it again to now see the statement after the complex expression is not executed

Branching alternatives

The **else** keyword is used in conjunction with the **if** keyword to create **if else** statements that provide alternative branches for a program to pursue – according to the evaluation of a tested expression. In its simplest form, this merely nominates an alternative statement for execution when the test fails:

if (*test-expression*)
    code-to-be-executed-when-true ;
else
    code-to-be-executed-when-false ;

Notice that the first statement is terminated with a semicolon, as usual, before the else keyword.

Each alternative branch may be a single statement or a statement block of multiple statements – enclosed within curly brackets.

More powerful **if else** statements can be constructed that evaluate a test expression for each alternative branch. These employ nested **if** statements after each **else** keyword to specify each further test. When the program discovers an expression that evaluates as **true**, it executes the statements associated with just that test then exits the **if else** statement without exploring any further branches:

Else.java

1. Start a new program named "Else" containing the standard main method

```
class Else
{
        public static void main ( String[] args ) {          }
}
```

2. Inside the main method, insert this line to declare and initialize an integer variable named **hrs**

```
int hrs = 11 ;
```

3. Insert this simple conditional test, which executes a single statement when the value of the **hrs** variable is below 13

```
if ( hrs < 13 )
{
        System.out.println( "Good morning: " + hrs ) ;
}
```

4. Save the program as **Else.java** then compile and run the program to see the statement get executed

```
Command Prompt
C:\MyJava> javac Else.java

C:\MyJava> java Else
Good morning: 11
```

5. Change the value assigned to the **hrs** variable to 15, then add this alternative branch right after the **if** statement

```
else if ( hrs < 18 )
{
        System.out.println( "Good afternoon: " + hrs ) ;
}
```

6. Save the changes, recompile, and run the program again to see just the alternative statement get executed

```
Command Prompt
C:\MyJava> javac Else.java

C:\MyJava> java Else
Good afternoon: 15
```

It is sometimes desirable to provide a final **else** branch, without a nested **if** statement, to specify a "default" statement to be executed when no tested expression evaluates as **true**:

7. Change the value assigned to the **hrs** variable to 21, then add this default branch to the end of the **if else** statement

```
else System.out.println( "Good evening: " + hrs ) ;
```

8. Save the changes, recompile, and run the program once more to see just the default statement get executed

```
Command Prompt
C:\MyJava> javac Else.java

C:\MyJava> java Else
Good evening: 21

C:\MyJava>
```

Conditional branching is the fundamental process by which computer programs proceed.

Switching branches

Lengthy **if else** statements, which offer many conditional branches for a program to pursue, can become unwieldy. Where the test expressions repeatedly evaluate the same variable value, a more elegant solution is often provided by a **switch** statement.

The syntax of a typical switch statement block looks like this:

```
switch ( test-variable )
{
        case value1 : code-to-be-executed-when-true ; break ;
        case value2 : code-to-be-executed-when-true ; break ;
        case value3 : code-to-be-executed-when-true ; break ;
        default : code-to-be-executed-when-false ;
}
```

The **switch** statement works in an unusual way. It takes a specified variable then seeks to match its assigned value from among a number of **case** options. Statements associated with the option whose value matches are then executed.

Optionally, a **switch** statement can include a final option using the **default** keyword to specify statements to execute when no case options match the value assigned to the specified variable.

Each option begins with the **case** keyword and a value to match. This is followed by a : colon character and the statements, if any, to be executed when the match is made.

Missing break keywords are not syntax errors – ensure that all intended breaks are present in switch blocks to avoid unexpected results.

It is important to recognize that the statement, or statement block, associated with each **case** option must be terminated by the **break** keyword. Otherwise, the program will continue to execute the statements of other **case** options after the matched option. Sometimes, this is desirable to specify a number of **case** options that should each execute the same statements if matched – for example, one statement for each block of three options, like this:

```
switch ( test-variable )
{
        case value1 : case value2 : case value3 :
                code-A-to-be-executed-when-true ; break ;

        case value4 : case value5 : case value6 :
                code-B-to-be-executed-when-true ; break ;
}
```

1. Start a new program named "Switch" containing the standard main method

```
class Switch
{
        public static void main ( String[] args ) {          }
}
```

Switch.java

2. Inside the main method, declare and initialize three integer variables

```
int month = 2, year = 2022, num = 31 ;
```

3. Add a switch statement block to test the value assigned to the **month** variable

```
switch ( month )
{

}
```

Notice how all three integer variables are declared and initialized inline here using convenient shorthand.

4. Inside the switch block, insert **case** options assigning a new value to the **num** variable for months 4, 6, 9 and 11

```
case 4 : case 6 : case 9 : case 11 : num = 30 ; break ;
```

5. Insert a **case** option assigning a new value to the **num** variable for month 2, according to the **year** value

```
case 2 : num = ( year % 4 == 0 ) ? 29 : 28 ; break ;
```

The conditional operator is used to good effect in Step 5. You can check back to page 34 to be reminded how it works.

6. After the switch block, at the end of the main method, add this line to output all three integer values

```
System.out.println( month+"/"+year+": "+num+"days" ) ;
```

7. Save the program as **Switch.java** then compile and run the program to see the output

```
Command Prompt
C:\MyJava> javac Switch.java

C:\MyJava> java Switch
2/2022: 28days

C:\MyJava>
```

Looping for

A loop is a block of code that repeatedly executes the statements it contains until a tested condition is met – then the loop ends and the program proceeds on to its next task.

The most frequently-used loop structure in Java programming employs the **for** keyword and has this syntax:

```
for ( initializer ; test-expression ; updater )
{
        statements-to-be-executed-on-each-iteration ;
}
```

The parentheses after the **for** keyword must contain three controls that establish the performance of the loop:

- **Initializer** – assigns an initial value to a counter variable, which will keep count of the number of iterations made by this loop. The variable for this purpose may be declared here, and it is traditionally a "trivial" integer variable named **i**.
- **Test expression** – evaluated at the start of each iteration of the loop for a Boolean **true** value. When the evaluation returns **true** the iteration proceeds but when it returns **false** the loop is immediately terminated, without completing that iteration.
- **Updater** – changes the current value of the counter variable, started by the initializer, keeping the running total of the number of iterations made by this loop. Typically, this will use **i++** for counting up, or **i--** for counting down.

The updater is often referred to as the "incrementer" as it more often increments, rather than decrements, the counter variable.

The code executed on each iteration of the loop can be a single statement, a statement block, or even another "nested" loop.

Every loop must, at some point, enable the test expression to return **false** – otherwise, an infinite loop is created that will relentlessly execute its statements. Commonly, the test expression will evaluate the current value of the counter variable to perform a specified number of iterations. For example, with a counter **i** initialized at one and incremented by one on each iteration, a test expression of **i < 11** becomes false after 10 iterations – so that loop will execute its statements 10 times before the loop ends.

For.java

1. Start a new program named "For" containing the standard main method

```
class For
{
        public static void main ( String[] args ) {          }
}
```

2. Inside the main method, declare and initialize an integer variable to count the total overall number of iterations

```
int num = 0 ;
```

3. Add a **for** loop to perform three iterations and display the current value of its counter variable **i** on each iteration

```
for ( int i = 1 ; i < 4 ; i++ )
{
        System.out.println( "Outer Loop i=" + i  ) ;
}
```

4. Inside the **for** loop block insert a nested **for** loop to also perform three iterations, displaying the current value of its counter variable **j** and total overall number of iterations

```
for ( int j = 1 ; j < 4 ; j++ )
{
        System.out.print( "\tInner Loop j=" + j ) ;
        System.out.println( "\t\tTotal num="+ (++num) ) ;
}
```

5. Save the program as **For.java** then compile and run the program to see the output

```
Command Prompt

C:\MyJava> javac For.java

C:\MyJava> java For
Outer Loop i=1
        Inner Loop j=1          Total num=1
        Inner Loop j=2          Total num=2
        Inner Loop j=3          Total num=3
Outer Loop i=2
        Inner Loop j=1          Total num=4
        Inner Loop j=2          Total num=5
        Inner Loop j=3          Total num=6
Outer Loop i=3
        Inner Loop j=1          Total num=7
        Inner Loop j=2          Total num=8
        Inner Loop j=3          Total num=9

C:\MyJava>
```

The increment **++** and decrement **--** operators can prefix a variable, to change its value immediately, or postfix the variable – so its value becomes changed when next referenced. Try changing the increment operators in this example to **++i** and **++j** to see the difference.

Looping while true

An alternative loop structure to that of the **for** loop, described on page 50, employs the **while** keyword and has this syntax:

```
while ( test-expression )
{
        statements-to-be-executed-on-each-iteration ;
}
```

Like the **for** loop, a **while** loop repeatedly executes the statements it contains until a tested condition is met – then the loop ends and the program proceeds on to its next task.

Unlike the **for** loop, the parentheses after the **while** keyword do not contain an initializer or updater for an iteration counter variable. This means that the test expression must evaluate some value that gets changed in the loop statements as the loop proceeds – otherwise, an infinite loop is created that will relentlessly execute its statements.

The test expression is evaluated at the start of each iteration of the loop for a Boolean **true** value. When the evaluation returns **true** the iteration proceeds, but when it returns **false** the loop is immediately terminated, without completing that iteration.

Note that if the test expression returns **false** when it is first evaluated, the loop statements are never executed.

An infinite loop will lock the program as it continues to perform iterations – on Windows, press **Ctrl + C** to halt.

A **while** loop can be made to resemble the structure of a **for** loop, to evaluate a counter variable in its test expression, by creating a counter variable outside the loop and changing its value within the statements it executes on each iteration. For example, the outer **for** loop in the previous example can be recreated as a **while** loop, like this:

```
int i = 1 ;

while ( i < 4 )
{
        System.out.println( "Outer Loop i=" +i ) ;
        i++ ;
}
```

This positions the counter initializer externally, before the while loop structure, and its updater within the statement block.

1. Start a new program named "While" containing the standard main method

```
class While
{
        public static void main ( String[] args ) {          }
}
```

While.java

2. Inside the main method, declare and initialize an integer variable named **num**

```
int num = 100 ;
```

3. Add a **while** loop to display the **num** variable's current value while it remains above zero

```
while ( num > 0 )
{
        System.out.println( "While Countdown: " + num ) ;
}
```

4. Insert an updater at the end of the **while** loop block to decrease the **num** variable's value by 10 on each iteration – thereby avoiding an infinite loop

```
num -= 10 ;
```

The assignment in this updater is shorthand for **num = (num - 10)**.

5. Save the program as **While.java** then compile and run the program to see the output

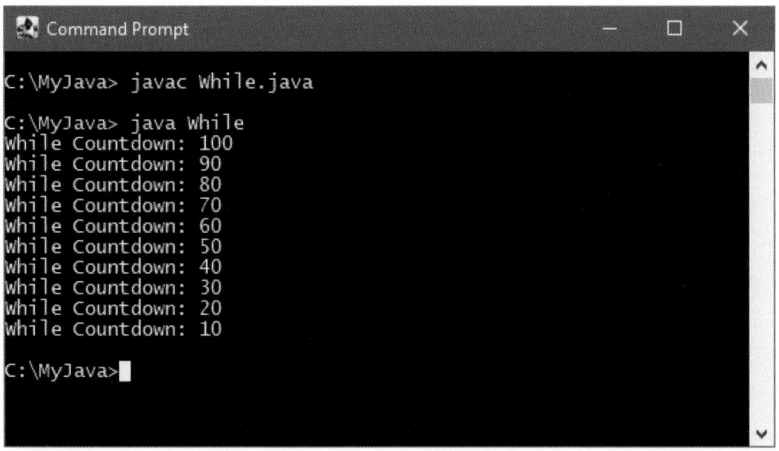

Doing do-while loops

A variation of the **while** loop structure, described on page 52, employs the **do** keyword to create a loop with this syntax:

```
do
{
        statements-to-be-executed-on-each-iteration ;
}
while ( test-expression ) ;
```

Like the **for** loop and **while** loop, a **do while** loop repeatedly executes the statements it contains until a tested condition is met – then the loop ends and the program proceeds to its next task.

Unlike the **for** loop and **while** loop, the **do while** test expression appears after the block containing the statements to be executed. The test expression is evaluated at the end of each iteration of the loop for a Boolean **true** value. When the evaluation returns **true** the next iteration proceeds, but when it returns **false** the loop is immediately terminated. This means that the statements in a **do while** loop are always executed at least once.

Note that if the test expression returns **false** when it is first evaluated, the loop statements have already been executed once.

A **do while** loop can be made to resemble the structure of a **for** loop, to evaluate a counter variable in its test expression, by positioning the counter initializer outside the loop structure and its updater within the statement block – just as with a **while** loop.

All **for**, **while**, or **do while** loop structures containing just one statement to execute may, optionally, omit the curly brackets around the statement. But, if omitted, you will need to add curly brackets if additional statements are added to the loop later.

Always enclose the statements to be executed by a loop within curly brackets – for clarity and improved code maintainability.

The choice of **for**, **while**, or **do while** loop is largely a matter of personal coding preference and purpose. A **for** loop structure conveniently locates the counter initializer, test expression, and updater in the parentheses after the **for** keyword. A **while** loop structure can be more concise – but you must remember to include an updater in the loop's statements to avoid an infinite loop. A **do while** loop simply adds the benefit of executing its statements once before evaluating its test expression – demonstrated by the **do while** loop described opposite.

1. Start a new program named "DoWhile" containing the standard main method

```
class DoWhile
{
        public static void main ( String[] args ) {          }
}
```

DoWhile.java

2. Inside the main method, declare and initialize an integer variable named **num**

```
int num = 100 ;
```

3. Add a **do while** loop to display the **num** variable's current value while it is below 10

```
do
{
        System.out.println( "DoWhile Countup: " + num ) ;
}
while ( num < 10 ) ;
```

4. Insert an updater at the end of the **do while** loop block to change the **num** variable's value on each iteration – thereby avoiding an infinite loop

```
num += 10 ;
```

The assignment in this updater is shorthand for **num = (num + 10)**.

5. Save the program as **DoWhile.java** then compile and run the program – see that the **num** variable never meets the test condition, but the statement executes once anyway

```
C:\MyJava> javac DoWhile.java

C:\MyJava> java DoWhile
DoWhile Countup: 100

C:\MyJava>
```

Breaking out of loops

The **break** keyword can be used to prematurely terminate a loop when a specified condition is met. The **break** statement is situated inside the loop statement block, and is preceded by a test expression. When the test returns **true**, the loop ends immediately and the program proceeds on to its next task. For example, in a nested loop it proceeds to the next iteration of its outer loop.

Break.java

1. Start a new program named "Break" containing the standard main method

```
class Break
{
        public static void main ( String[] args ) {          }
}
```

2. Inside the main method, create two nested **for** loops that display their counter values on each of three iterations

```
for ( int i = 1 ; i < 4 ; i++ )
{
        for ( int j = 1 ; j < 4 ; j++ )
        {
           System.out.println( "Running i="+i+" j="+j ) ;
        }
}
```

3. Save the program as **Break.java** then compile and run the program to see the output

```
Command Prompt

C:\MyJava> javac Break.java

C:\MyJava> java Break
Running i=1 j=1
Running i=1 j=2
Running i=1 j=3
Running i=2 j=1
Running i=2 j=2
Running i=2 j=3
Running i=3 j=1
Running i=3 j=2
Running i=3 j=3
```

This program makes three iterations of the outer loop, which executes the inner loop on each iteration. A **break** statement can be added to stop the second execution of the inner loop.

4 Add this **break** statement to the beginning of the inner loop statement block, to break out of the inner loop – then recompile and re-run the program

```
if ( i == 2 && j == 1 )
{
        System.out.println( "Breaks innerLoop
                                when i=" +i+ " j=" +j ) ;

        break ;
}
```

Here, the **break** statement halts all three iterations of the inner loop when the outer loop tries to run it the second time.

```
Command Prompt
C:\MyJava> javac Break.java

C:\MyJava> java Break
Running i=1 j=1
Running i=1 j=2
Running i=1 j=3
Breaks innerLoop when i=2 j=1
Running i=3 j=1
Running i=3 j=2
Running i=3 j=3
```

The **continue** keyword can be used to skip a single iteration of a loop when a specified condition is met. The **continue** statement is situated inside the loop statement block and is preceded by a test expression. When the test returns **true**, that iteration ends.

5 Add this **continue** statement to the beginning of the inner loop statement block, to skip the first iteration of the inner loop – then recompile and re-run the program

```
if ( i == 1 && j == 1 )
{
        System.out.println( "Continues innerLoop
                                when i=" +i+ " j=" +j ) ;
        continue;
}
```

Here, the **continue** statement skips just the first iteration of the inner loop when the outer loop tries to run it for the first time.

```
Command Prompt
C:\MyJava> javac Break.java

C:\MyJava> java Break
Continues innerLoop when i=1 j=1
Running i=1 j=2
Running i=1 j=3
Breaks innerLoop when i=2 j=1
Running i=3 j=1
Running i=3 j=2
Running i=3 j=3
```

Returning control

The default behavior of the **break** and **continue** keywords can be changed to explicitly specify that control should return to a labeled outer loop by stating its label name. This allows a loop to perform iterations until a specified condition is met or broken.

The syntax to label a loop requires a label name, followed by a : colon character, to precede the start of the loop structure.

Label.java

1. Start a new program named "Label" containing the standard main method

```
class Label
{
        public static void main ( String[] args ) {          }
}
```

2. Inside the main method, create two nested **for** loops that display their counter values on each of three iterations

```
for ( int i = 1 ; i < 4 ; i++ )
{
        for ( int j = 1 ; j < 4 ; j++ )
        {
           System.out.println( "Running i="+i+ " j="+j ) ;
        }
}
```

3. Save the program as **Label.java** then compile and run the program to see the output

```
Command Prompt
C:\MyJava> javac Label.java

C:\MyJava> java Label
Running i=1 j=1
Running i=1 j=2
Running i=1 j=3
Running i=2 j=1
Running i=2 j=2
Running i=2 j=3
Running i=3 j=1
Running i=3 j=2
Running i=3 j=3

C:\MyJava>
```

4. Edit the start of the outer loop to label it "outerLoop"

```
outerLoop : for ( int i = 1 ; i < 4 ; i++ )
```

To explicitly specify that the program should proceed in the outer loop, state that loop's label name after the **continue** keyword.

5 Add this **continue** statement to the beginning of the inner loop statement block, to proceed at the next iteration of the outer loop – then recompile and re-run the program

```
if ( i == 1 && j == 1 )
{
        System.out.println( "Continues outerLoop
                                when i=" +i+ " j=" +j ) ;
        continue outerLoop ;
}
```

Here the **continue** statement halts all three iterations of the inner loop's first run – by returning control to the outer loop.

```
Command Prompt
C:\MyJava> javac Label.java

C:\MyJava> java Label
Continues outerLoop when i=1 j=1
Running i=2 j=1
Running i=2 j=2
Running i=2 j=3
Running i=3 j=1
Running i=3 j=2
Running i=3 j=3
```

To explicitly specify that the program should exit from the outer loop, state that loop's label name after the **break** keyword.

6 Add this **break** statement to the beginning of the inner loop statement block, to exit the outer loop – then recompile and re-run the program

```
if ( i == 2 && j == 3 )
{
        System.out.println( "Breaks outerLoop
                                when i=" +i+ " j=" +j ) ;
        break outerLoop ;
}
```

Here the **break** statement halts all further iterations of the entire loop structure – by exiting from the outer loop.

```
Select Command Prompt
C:\MyJava> javac Label.java

C:\MyJava> java Label
Continues outerLoop when i=1 j=1
Running i=2 j=1
Running i=2 j=2
Breaks outerLoop when i=2 j=3
```

Summary

- The **if** keyword performs a conditional test to evaluate an expression for a Boolean value of **true** or **false**.
- An **if** statement block can contain one or more statements, which are only executed when the test expression returns **true**.
- The **else** keyword specifies alternative statements to execute when the test performed by the **if** keyword returns **false**.
- Combined **if else** statements enable a program to proceed by the process of conditional branching.
- A **switch** statement can often provide an elegant solution to unwieldy **if else** statements by offering **case** options.
- Each **case** option can be terminated by the **break** keyword so only statements associated with that option will be executed.
- The **default** keyword can specify statements to be executed when all **case** options return **false**.
- A loop repeatedly executes the statements it contains until a tested expression returns **false**.
- The parentheses that follow the **for** keyword specify the loop's counter initializer, test expression, and counter updater.
- Statements in a **while** loop and a **do while** loop must change a value used in their test expression to avoid an infinite loop.
- The test expression is evaluated at the start of **for** loops and **while** loops – before the first iteration of the loop.
- The test expression is evaluated at the end of **do while** loops – after the first iteration of the loop.
- A loop iteration can be skipped using the **continue** keyword.
- A loop can be terminated using the **break** keyword.
- Nested inner loops can use labels with the **break** and **continue** keywords to reference the outer loop.

4 Directing values

This chapter demonstrates how to direct data values using various Java programming constructs.

62 Casting type values

64 Creating variable arrays

66 Passing an argument

68 Passing multiple arguments

70 Looping through elements

72 Changing element values

74 Adding array dimensions

76 Catching exceptions

78 Summary

Casting type values

Handling values in Java programming requires correct data typing to be closely observed to avoid compiler errors. For example, sending a **float** type value to a method that requires an **int** type value will produce a compiler error. This means it is often necessary to convert a value to another data type before it can be processed.

Numeric values can be easily "cast" (converted) into another numeric data type using this syntax:

(*data-type*) *value*

Some loss of precision will occur when casting **float** floating point values into an **int** data type, as the number will be truncated at the decimal point. For example, casting a **float** value of 9.9 into an **int** variable produces an integer value of nine.

Interestingly, character values of the **char** data type can automatically be used as **int** values because they each have a unique integer representation. This is their numeric code value in the ASCII character set, which is supported by Java. The uppercase letter A, for instance, has the code value of 65.

Numeric values can be converted to the **String** data type using the **toString()** method of that value's data type class. This takes the numeric value as its argument, within the parentheses. For example, convert an **int num** variable to a **String** with **Integer.toString(num)**. Similarly, convert a **float num** variable to a **String** with **Float.toString(num)**. In practice, this technique is not always required because Java automatically converts concatenated variables to a **String** if any one of the variables has a **String** value.

All numeric classes have a **parse...** method and a **toString** method allowing conversion between **String** values and numeric data types.

More frequently, you will want to convert a **String** value to a numeric data type so the program can use that value arithmetically. A **String** value can be converted to an **int** value using the **Integer.parseInt()** method. This takes the **String** value as its argument, within the parentheses. For example, convert a **String msg** variable to an **int** with **Integer.parseInt(msg)**. Similarly, convert a **String msg** variable to a **float** with **Float.parseFloat(msg)**. When converting a **String** value to a numeric data type, the **String** may only contain a valid numeric value, or the compiler will report an error.

Convert.java

1. Start a new program named "Convert" containing the standard main method

```
class Convert
{
        public static void main ( String[] args ) {          }
}
```

2. Inside the main method, declare and initialize a **float** variable and a **String** variable

```
float daysFloat = 365.25f ;
String weeksString = "52" ;
```

3. Cast the **float** value into an **int** variable

```
int daysInt = (int) daysFloat ;
```

4. Convert the **String** value into an **int** variable

```
int weeksInt = Integer.parseInt( weeksString ) ;
```

5. Perform arithmetic on the converted values and display the result

```
int week = ( daysInt / weeksInt ) ;
System.out.println( "Days per week: " + week ) ;
```

6. Save the program as **Convert.java** then compile and run the program to see the output

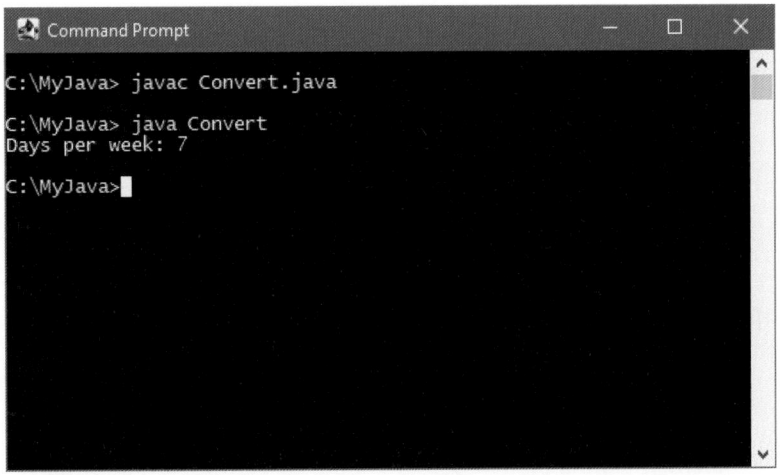

Creating variable arrays

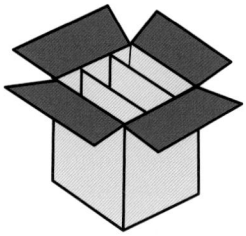

An array is simply a variable that can contain multiple values – unlike a regular variable that can only contain a single value.

The declaration of an array first states its data type, using one of the data type keywords, followed by square brackets [ ] to denote that it will be an array variable. Next, the declaration states the array variable name, adhering to the normal naming conventions.

An array can be initialized in its declaration by assigning values of the appropriate data type as a comma-delimited list, enclosed within curly brackets. For example, the declaration of an integer array variable initialized with three values might look like this:

```
int[] numbersArray = { 1, 2, 3 } ;
```

The array is created of the length of the assigned list, allowing one "element" per value – in this case, an array of three elements.

Stored values are indexed starting at zero, and each value can be addressed by its element index position. The syntax to do so requires the array name to be followed by square brackets containing the element index. For instance, **numbersArray[0]** would address the first value stored in the example above (1).

Although the values stored in each element can be changed as simply as those of regular variables, the size of an array is determined by its declaration and cannot be changed later. Usefully, the total number of elements in an array is stored as an integer in the **length** property of that array. The syntax to address this figure just tacks a period and "length" onto the array name. For example, **numbersArray.length** would return the size of the array in the example above – in this case, the integer 3.

Remember that array indexing starts at zero. This means that **index[2]** addresses the third element in the array, not its second element.

Arrays can also be declared without assigning a list of initial values by using the **new** keyword to create an empty array "object" of a specified size. The number of required empty elements is stated in the assignment within square brackets after the appropriate data type. For example, the declaration of an empty integer array variable with three elements might look like this:

```
int[] numbersArray = new int[3] ;
```

The elements are assigned default values of zero for **int** and **float** data types, **null** for **String** data types, **\0** for **char** data types, and **false** for **boolean** data types.

1. Start a new program named "Array" containing the standard main method

```
class Array
{
        public static void main ( String[] args ) {        }
}
```

Array.java

2. Inside the main method, declare and initialize a **String** array with three elements

```
String[] str = { "Much ", "More", " Java" } ;
```

3. Declare an empty integer array with three elements

```
int[] num = new int[3] ;
```

4. Assign values to the first two integer array elements

```
num[0] = 100 ;
num[1] = 200 ;
```

5. Assign a new value to the second String array element

```
str[1] = "Better" ;
```

6. Output the length of each array and the content of all elements in each array

```
System.out.println( "String array length is " + str.length ) ;
System.out.println( "Integer array length is "+ num.length) ;
System.out.println( num[0] + "," +num[1]+ ","+num[2] ) ;
System.out.println( str[0] + str[1] + str[2] ) ;
```

7. Save the program as **Array.java** then compile and run the program to see the output

String values need to be enclosed within quotes.

```
Command Prompt

C:\MyJava> javac Array.java

C:\MyJava> java Array
String array length is 3
Integer array length is 3
100,200,0
Much Better Java

C:\MyJava>
```

Passing an argument

The standard Java code that declares the program's **main** method includes an argument within its parentheses that creates a **String** array, traditionally named "args":

```
public static void main( String[] args ) { }
```

The purpose of the **args[]** array is to allow values to be passed to the program when it is called upon to run. At the command line, a value to be passed to the program is added after a single space following the program name. For example, the command to pass the **String** "Java" to a program named "Run" would be **Run Java**.

A single value passed to a program is automatically placed into the first element of the **args[]** array, so it can be addressed by the program as **args[0]**.

It is important to recognize that the **args[]** array is of the **String** data type – so a numeric value passed to a program will be stored as a **String** representation of that number. This means that the program cannot use that value arithmetically until it has been converted to a numerical data type, such as an **int** value. For example, **Run 4** passes the number four to the program, which stores it as the **String "4"**, not as the **int 4**. Consequently, output of **args[0]+3** produces the concatenated **String** "43", not the sum 7. The argument can be converted with the **Integer.parseInt()** method so that **Integer.parseInt(args[0])+3** does produce the sum 7.

A **String** containing spaces can be passed to a program as a single **String** value by enclosing the entire **String** within double quotes on the command line. For example, **Run "Java in easy steps"**.

Passing an argument to a program is most useful to determine how the program should run by indicating an execution option. The option is passed to the program as a **String** value in **args[0]** and can be evaluated using the **String.equals()** method. The syntax for this just tacks a period and "equals()" onto the array name, with a comparison **String** within the parentheses. For example, **args[0].equals("b")** evaluates the argument for the **String** value "b".

1. Start a new program named "Option" containing the standard main method

```
class Option
{
        public static void main ( String[] args ) {          }
}
```

Option.java

2. Inside the main method, write an **if** statement to seek an argument of "-en"

```
if ( args[0].equals( "-en" ) )
{
        System.out.println( "English option" ) ;
}
```

3. Add an **else** alternative onto the **if** statement to seek an argument of "-es"

```
else if ( args[0].equals( "-es" ) )
{
        System.out.println( "Spanish option" ) ;
}
```

4. Add another **else** alternative onto the **if** statement to provide a default response

```
else System.out.println( "Unrecognized option" ) ;
```

5. Save the program as **Option.java** then compile and run the program to see the output

```
Command Prompt

C:\MyJava> javac Option.java

C:\MyJava> java Option -en
English option

C:\MyJava> java Option -es
Spanish option

C:\MyJava> java Option -ez
Unrecognized option

C:\MyJava>
```

This example will throw an **ArrayIndexOutOfBounds** exception if you attempt to execute the program without any argument. See page 76 for details on how to catch exceptions.

Passing multiple arguments

Multiple arguments can be passed to a program at the command line, following the program name and a space. The arguments must be separated by at least one space and their values are placed, in order, into the elements of the **args[]** array. Each value can then be addressed by its index number as with any other array – **args[0]** for the first argument, **args[1]** for the second argument, and so on.

The program can test the **length** property of the **args[]** array to ensure the user has entered the appropriate number of arguments. When the test fails, the **return** keyword can be used to exit the **main** method, thereby exiting the program:

Args.java

1. Start a new program named "Args" containing the standard main method

```
class Args
{
        public static void main ( String[] args ) {          }
}
```

2. Inside the main method, write an **if** statement to output advice and exit the program when there are not the required number of arguments – in this case, three

```
if ( args.length != 3 )
{
   System.out.println( "Wrong number of arguments" ) ;
   return ;
}
```

3. Below the **if** statement, create two **int** variables – initialized with the values of the first argument and third argument respectively

```
int num1 = Integer.parseInt( args[0] ) ;
int num2 = Integer.parseInt( args[2] ) ;
```

4. Add a **String** variable, initialized with a concatenation of all three arguments

```
String msg = args[0] + args[1] + args[2] + "=" ;
```

The **return** keyword exits the current method. It can also return a value to the point where the method was called. See page 99 for more details.

5. Add this **if else** statement to perform arithmetic on the arguments and append the result to the **String** variable

```
if ( args[1].equals("+") )          msg += (num1 + num2);
else if ( args[1].equals("-") )     msg += (num1 - num2) ;
else if ( args[1].equals("x") )     msg += (num1 * num2) ;
else if ( args[1].equals("/") )     msg += (num1 / num2) ;
else msg = "Incorrect operator" ;
```

6. Insert this line at the end of the main method to display the appended **String**

```
System.out.println( msg ) ;
```

7. Save the program as **Args.java** then compile and run the program with three arguments – an integer, any arithmetical symbol + - x /, and another integer

```
Command Prompt

C:\MyJava> javac Args.java

C:\MyJava> java Args 16 + 4
16+4=20

C:\MyJava> java Args 16 - 4
16-4=12

C:\MyJava> java Args 16 x 4
16x4=64

C:\MyJava> java Args 16 / 4
16/4=4

C:\MyJava>
```

8. Now, run the program with an incorrect second argument and with the wrong number of arguments

```
Command Prompt

C:\MyJava> java Args 16 % 4
Incorrect operator

C:\MyJava> java Args 16 +
Wrong number of arguments

C:\MyJava>
```

This program will report an error if non-numeric values are entered. See page 76 for details on how to catch errors.

Looping through elements

All types of loop can be used to easily read all the values stored inside the elements of an array. The loop counter should start with the index number of the first element then proceed on up to the final index number. The index number of the last element in an array will always be one less than the array length – because the index starts at zero.

It is useful to set the array **length** property as the loop's conditional test determining when the loop should end. This means that the loop will continue until the counter value exceeds the index number of the array's final element.

Loops.java

1. Start a new program named "Loops" containing the standard main method

```
class Loops
{
        public static void main ( String[] args ) {          }
}
```

2. Inside the main method, write an **if** statement to test whether any argument values have been entered into the **args[]** array from the command line

```
if ( args.length > 0 ) {   }
```

3. Insert a **for** loop inside the curly brackets of the **if** statement to output the value stored in each element

```
for ( int i = 0 ; i < args.length ; i++ )
{
        System.out.println( "args[" +i+ "] is | "+ args[i] ) ;
}
```

4. Save the program as **Loops.java** then compile the program and run it with the arguments **Java in easy steps**

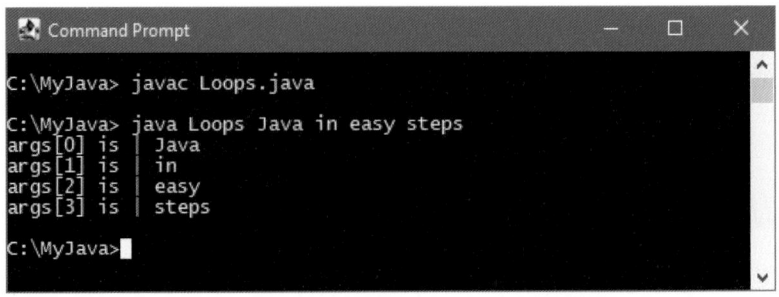

5. Edit **Loops.java** to add a **String** array and a **while** loop to output the value stored in each element

```
String[] htm = { "HTML", "in", "easy", "steps" } ;

int j = 0 ;
while ( j < htm.length )
{
        System.out.println( "htm[" +j+ "] is | " + htm[j] ) ;
        j++ ;
}
```

6. Save the changes, then recompile and re-run the program

```
Command Prompt
C:\MyJava> javac Loops.java

C:\MyJava> java Loops
htm[0] is | HTML
htm[1] is | in
htm[2] is | easy
htm[3] is | steps
```

7. Edit **Loops.java** to add another **String** array and a **do while** loop to output the value stored in each element

```
String[] xml = { "XML", "in", "easy", "steps" } ;

int k = 0 ;
if ( xml.length > 0 ) do
{
        System.out.println( "\t\txml["+k+"] is | "+xml[k] ) ;
        k++ ;
} while ( k < xml.length ) ;
```

8. Save the changes, then recompile and re-run the program

```
Command Prompt
C:\MyJava> javac Loops.java

C:\MyJava> java Loops
htm[0] is | HTML
htm[1] is | in
htm[2] is | easy
htm[3] is | steps
            xml[0] is | XML
            xml[1] is | in
            xml[2] is | easy
            xml[3] is | steps
```

Notice that the **do** statement is preceded by a conditional test to ensure the array is not empty before attempting to output the value of the first element.

Changing element values

The value stored in an array element can be changed by assigning a new value to that particular element using its index number. Additionally, any type of loop can be used to efficiently populate all the elements in an array from values stored in other arrays.

This ability is especially useful to combine data from multiple arrays into a single array of totaled data.

Elements.java

1. Start a new program named "Elements" containing the standard main method

```
class Elements
{
        public static void main ( String[] args ) {          }
}
```

2. In the main method, add initialized **int** arrays representing monthly kiosk sales from all four quarters of a year

```
int[] kiosk_q1  = { 42000 , 48000 , 50000 } ;
int[] kiosk_q2  = { 52000 , 58000 , 60000 } ;
int[] kiosk_q3  = { 46000 , 49000 , 58000 } ;
int[] kiosk_q4  = { 50000 , 51000 , 61000 } ;
```

3. Add initialized **int** arrays representing monthly outlet sales from all four quarters of a year

```
int[] outlet_q1 = { 57000 , 63000 , 60000 } ;
int[] outlet_q2 = { 70000 , 67000 , 73000 } ;
int[] outlet_q3 = { 67000 , 65000 , 62000 } ;
int[] outlet_q4 = { 72000 , 69000 , 75000 } ;
```

4. Now, create an empty **int** array of 12 elements in which to combine all the monthly sales figures and an **int** variable in which to record their grand total value

```
int[] sum = new int[ 12 ] ;
int total = 0 ;
```

5. Add a **for** loop to populate each element of the empty array with combined values from the other arrays

```
for ( int i = 0 ; i < kiosk_q1.length ; i++ )
{
        sum[ i ]   = kiosk_q1[i] + outlet_q1[i] ;
        sum[i+3] = kiosk_q2[i] + outlet_q2[i] ;
        sum[i+6] = kiosk_q3[i] + outlet_q3[i] ;
        sum[i+9] = kiosk_q4[i] + outlet_q4[i] ;
}
```

6. Next, add a second **for** loop to output each of the combined monthly sales totals, and to calculate their grand total

```
for ( int i = 0 ; i < sum.length ; i++ )
{
        System.out.println( "Month "+ ( i+1 ) +
                                    " sales:\t" + sum[i] ) ;
        total += sum[i] ;
}
```

The counter number gets increased by one to produce the month numbers 1-12.

7. Insert a final statement at the end of the main method to output the grand total

```
System.out.println( "TOTAL YEAR SALES\t" + total ) ;
```

8. Save the program as **Elements.java** then compile the program and run it to see the output

```
Command Prompt

C:\MyJava> javac Elements.java

C:\MyJava> java Elements
Month 1 sales:  99000
Month 2 sales:  111000
Month 3 sales:  110000
Month 4 sales:  122000
Month 5 sales:  125000
Month 6 sales:  133000
Month 7 sales:  113000
Month 8 sales:  114000
Month 9 sales:  120000
Month 10 sales: 122000
Month 11 sales: 120000
Month 12 sales: 136000
TOTAL YEAR SALES        1425000

C:\MyJava>
```

Adding array dimensions

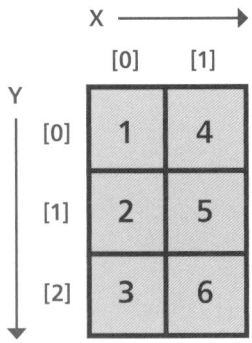

Arrays can be created to store multiple sets of element values, each having their own index dimension. Individual values are addressed in a multi-dimensional array using the appropriate index numbers of each dimension – for example, **num [1] [3]**.

A two-dimensional array might be used to record an integer value for each day of a business year, organized by week. This requires an array of 52 elements (one per week) that each have an array of seven elements (one per day). Its declaration looks like this:

```
int[][] dailyRecord = new int [52] [7] ;
```

This "array of arrays" provides an element for each business day. Values are assigned to a multi-dimensional array by stating the appropriate index numbers of each dimension. With the example above, for instance, a value can be assigned to the first day of the sixth week, like this:

```
dailyRecord [5] [0] = 5000 ;
```

Each array has its own **length** property that can be accessed by specifying the dimension required. For the example above, the syntax **dailyRecord.length** returns a value of 52 – the size of the first dimension. To access the size of the second dimension, the syntax **dailyRecord[0].length** returns the value of seven.

Avoid using more than three dimensions in arrays – it will be confusing.

Two-dimensional arrays are often used to store grid coordinates, where one dimension represents the X axis and the other dimension represents the Y axis – for example, **point[3][5]**.

Three-dimensional arrays can be used to store XYZ coordinates in a similar way, but it can be difficult to visualize **point[4][8][2]**.

Nested loops are perfectly suited to multi-dimensional arrays, as each loop level can address the elements of each array dimension.

Dimensions.java

1. Start a new program named "Dimensions" containing the standard main method

```
class Dimensions
{
        public static void main ( String[] args ) {          }
}
```

2. In the main method, create a two-dimensional array to store Boolean flats relating to XY coordinates
```
boolean[][] points = new boolean[5][20] ;
```

3. Define one Y point on each X axis
```
points[0][5] = true ;
points[1][6] = true ;
points[2][7] = true ;
points[3][8] = true ;
points[4][9] = true ;
```

Boolean variables are **false** by default.

4. Add a **for** loop to iterate through the first array index, adding a newline character at the end of each iteration
```
for ( int i = 0 ; i < points.length ; i++ )
{

        System.out.print( "\n" ) ;
}
```

5. Within the curly brackets of the **for** loop, insert a second **for** loop to iterate through the second array index
```
for ( int j = 0 ; j < points[0].length ; j++ ) {      }
```

6. Within the curly brackets of the second **for** loop, insert a statement to output a character for each element according to that element's Boolean value
```
char mark = ( points[i][j] ) ? 'X' : '-' ;
System.out.print( mark ) ;
```

7. Save the program as **Dimensions.java** then compile and run the program to see the output

```
Command Prompt
C:\MyJava> javac Dimensions.java

C:\MyJava> java Dimensions
-----X--------------
------X-------------
-------X------------
--------X-----------
---------X----------

C:\MyJava>
```

Catching exceptions

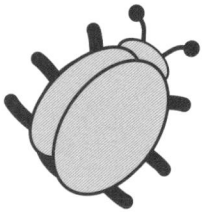

A program may encounter a runtime problem that causes an "exception" error, which halts its execution. Often, this will be created by unexpected user input. A well-written program should, therefore, attempt to anticipate all possible ways the user might cause exceptions at runtime.

Code where exceptions might arise can be identified and enclosed within a **try catch** statement block. This allows the program to handle exceptions without halting execution and looks like this:

```
try
{
        statements where an exception may arise
}
catch( Exception e )
{
        statements responding to an exception
}
```

The parentheses following the **catch** keyword specify the class of exception to be caught and assign it to the variable "e". The top-level **Exception** class catches all exceptions. Responses can be provided for specific exceptions, however, using multiple **catch** statements to identify different lower-level exception classes.

The most common exceptions are the **NumberFormatException**, which arises when the program encounters a value that is not of the expected numeric type, and the **ArrayIndexOutOfBoundsException**, which arises when the program attempts to address an array element number that is outside the index size. It is helpful to create a separate response for each of these exceptions to readily notify the user about the nature of the problem.

Optionally, a **try catch** statement block can be extended with a **finally** statement block, containing code that will always be executed – irrespective of whether the program has encountered exceptions.

The **e.getMessage()** method returns further information about some captured exceptions.

Exceptions.java

1. Start a new program named "Exceptions" containing the standard main method

```
class Exceptions
{
        public static void main ( String[] args ) {          }
}
```

2. Inside the main method, write a **try** statement to output a single integer argument

```
try
{
        int num = Integer.parseInt( args[0] ) ;
        System.out.println( "You entered: "+ num ) ;
}
```

3. Add a **catch** statement to handle the exception that arises when the program is run without an argument

```
catch( ArrayIndexOutOfBoundsException e )
{ System.out.println( "Integer argument required." ) ;    }
```

4. Add a **catch** statement to handle the exception that arises when the program is run with a non-integer argument

```
catch( NumberFormatException e )
{ System.out.println( "Argument is wrong format." ) ;    }
```

5. Add a **finally** statement at the end of the program

```
finally { System.out.println( "Program ends." ) ; }
```

6. Save the program as **Exceptions.java** then compile and run the program, trying to cause exceptions

```
Command Prompt

C:\MyJava> javac Exceptions.java

C:\MyJava> java Exceptions
Integer argument required.
Program ends.

C:\MyJava> java Exceptions TWENTY
Argument is wrong format.
Program ends.

C:\MyJava> java Exceptions 28
You entered: 28
Program ends.

C:\MyJava>
```

Summary

- Numeric values can be converted to other numeric data types by casting, and to the **String** type using the **toString()** method.
- A **String** value can be converted to an **int** value using the **Integer.parseInt()** method, and to a **float** using **Float.parseFloat()**.
- An array is a variable that can contain multiple values, initialized as a list within curly brackets in its declaration.
- An empty array object can be created using the **new** keyword.
- The **length** property of an array stores an integer, which is the number of elements in that array.
- Each element of an array can be addressed by its index number.
- A program's **main** method creates a **String** array, traditionally named "args", to store command line arguments.
- The first command line argument gets automatically stored in the **args[0]** element – as a **String** data type.
- Multiple arguments being passed to a program from the command line must each be separated by a space.
- Loops are an ideal way to read all the values stored within array elements.
- Data from multiple arrays can be combined to form a new array of totaled data in each element.
- Multi-dimensional arrays can store multiple sets of element values, each having their own index dimension.
- A **try catch** statement block is used to anticipate and handle runtime exceptions that may arise.
- The **Exception** class catches all exception errors, including **NumberFormatException** and **ArrayIndexOutOfBoundsException**.
- A **try catch** statement can be extended with a **finally** statement block, containing code that will always be executed.

5 Manipulating data

This chapter demonstrates how to manipulate program data using various Java library methods.

80 Exploring Java classes

82 Doing mathematics

84 Rounding numbers

86 Generating random numbers

88 Managing strings

90 Comparing strings

92 Searching strings

94 Manipulating characters

96 Summary

Exploring Java classes

Java has a vast library of pre-tested code packages, which are arranged in modules. Those providing functionality that is fundamental to the Java language itself are contained in the **java.lang** package, within the **java.base** module. These are automatically accessible to the Java API (Application Programming Interface). This means that the properties and methods provided by the **java.lang** package are readily available when creating programs. For example, the mathematic functionality provided by the **abs()** method of the **Math** class, which is part of the **java.lang** package, in the **java.base** module.

Package contents are arranged in hierarchical order, allowing any item to be addressed using dot notation. For example, the **System** class contains an **out** property (field), which in turn contains a **println()** method – so can be addressed as **System.out.println()**.

The Java documentation provides information about every item available, and can be used to explore the Java classes. It is available online via **docs.oracle.com/en/java** and can be downloaded for offline reference. The documentation is understandably large, but familiarity with it is valuable. A good starting point is the API Overview page containing a list of every module, together with a brief description of each module:

1. Browse to **docs.oracle.com/en/java** and click the link to **Java SE Technical Documentation**, then click **API Documentation**

2. See **All Modules** listed alphabetically – click the link for the **java.base** module (the foundational APIs of Java SE)

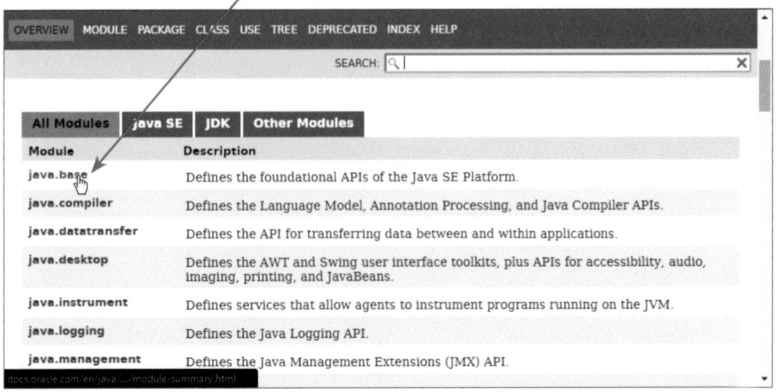

Modules were introduced to improve scalability and increase performance.

3 See the module's **Packages** listed alphabetically in each section – scroll down the page to the "Exports" section and click the link for the **java.lang** package

OVERVIEW MODULE PACKAGE CLASS USE TREE DEPRECATED INDEX HELP

MODULE: DESCRIPTION | MODULES | PACKAGES | SERVICES

SEARCH:

Packages

Exports

Package	Description
java.io	Provides for system input and output through data streams, serialization and the file system.
java.lang	Provides classes that are fundamental to the design of the Java programming language.

docs.oracle.com/en/java/.../package-summary.html

You can also use the Search box to find information on any item.

4 See the package's **Classes** listed alphabetically in each section – scroll down the page to the "Class Summary" section and click the link for the **Math** class

OVERVIEW MODULE PACKAGE CLASS USE TREE DEPRECATED INDEX HELP

SEARCH:

Integer	The Integer class wraps a value of the primitive type int in an object.
Long	The Long class wraps a value of the primitive type long in an object.
Math	The class Math contains methods for performing basic numeric operations such as the elementary exponential, logarithm, square root, and trigonometric functions.
Module	Represents a run-time module, either named or unnamed.

docs.oracle.com/en/java/.../Math.html

5 See the class's **Methods** listed alphabetically in the "Method Summary" section – to discover the purpose and syntax of any method simply click on its link

OVERVIEW MODULE PACKAGE CLASS USE TREE DEPRECATED INDEX HELP

SUMMARY: NESTED | FIELD | CONSTR | METHOD DETAIL: FIELD | CONSTR | METHOD

SEARCH: Search

Method Summary

All Methods | Static Methods | Concrete Methods

Modifier and Type	Method	Description
static double	abs(double a)	Returns the absolute value of a double value.

Examine the information available via other items on the page menu to become more familiar with the documentation.

Doing mathematics

The **Math** class within the **java.lang** package provides two constant values that are often useful to perform mathematical calculations. **Math.PI** stores the value of Pi, and **Math.E** stores the value that is the base of natural logarithms. Both these constant values are stored as **double** precision data types with 15 decimal places.

Pi.java

1. Start a new program named "Pi" containing the standard main method

```
class Pi
{
        public static void main ( String[] args ) {          }
}
```

2. Inside the main method, declare and initialize a **float** variable from a command line argument, and cast the **double Math.PI** constant into a second **float** variable

```
float radius = Float.parseFloat( args[0] ) ;
float shortPi = (float) Math.PI ;
```

3. Perform mathematical calculations using the cast value, assigning the results to more **float** variables

```
float circ = shortPi * ( radius + radius ) ;
float area = shortPi * ( radius * radius ) ;
```

4. Output the value of **Math.PI** and its cast **float** equivalent, followed by the results of the calculations

```
System.out.print( "With Pi commuted from " + Math.PI ) ;
System.out.println( " to " + shortPi + "..." ) ;
System.out.println( "A circle of radius " + radius + " cm" ) ;
System.out.println( "has a circumference of " + circ + " cm" ) ;
System.out.println( " and an area of " + area + " sq.cm" ) ;
```

5. Save the program as **Pi.java** then compile and run the program to see the output

The commuted value of Pi usually provides sufficient precision.

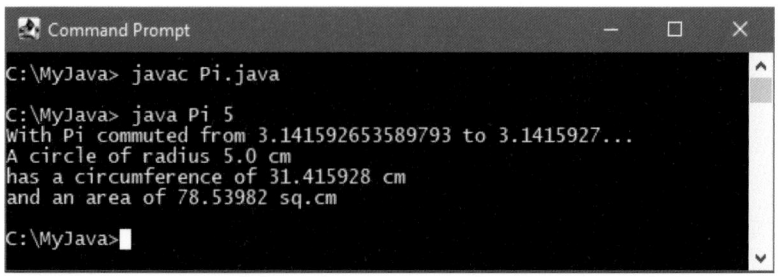

The **Math** class within the **java.lang** package provides many methods that are useful to perform mathematical calculations. Using **Math.pow()**, a given number can be raised to a specified power. The parentheses require the number as its first argument and the power by which it is to be raised as its second argument. The **Math.sqrt()** method returns the square root of the number specified as its sole argument. Both methods return a **double** type.

Power.java

1. Start a new program named "Power" containing the standard main method

```
class Power
{
        public static void main ( String[] args ) {          }
}
```

2. Inside the main method, declare and initialize an **int** variable from a passed command line argument

```
int num = Integer.parseInt( args[0] ) ;
```

3. Perform mathematical calculations, casting the results into more **int** variables

```
int square = (int) Math.pow( num , 2 ) ;
int cube = (int) Math.pow( num , 3 ) ;
int sqrt = (int) Math.sqrt( num ) ;
```

4. Output the results of the calculations

```
System.out.println( num + " squared is " + square ) ;
System.out.println( num + " cubed is " + cube ) ;
System.out.println( "Square root of " + num + " is "+ sqrt ) ;
```

5. Save the program as **Power.java** then compile and run the program to see the output

Both these examples could be improved by adding **try catch** statement blocks to anticipate user errors – see page 76 for details.

```
Command Prompt
C:\MyJava> javac Power.java

C:\MyJava> java Power 9
9 squared is 81
9 cubed is 729
Square root of 9 is 3

C:\MyJava>
```

Rounding numbers

The **Math** class within the **java.lang** package provides three methods to round floating-point numbers to the nearest integer. Simplest of these is the **Math.round()** method that rounds a number stated as its argument up, or down, to the closest integer.

The **Math.floor()** method rounds down to the closest integer below, and **Math.ceil()** rounds up to the closest integer above.

While the **Math.round()** method returns an **int** data type, both **Math.floor()** and **Math.ceil()** methods return a **double** data type.

Round.java

1. Start a new program named "Round" containing the standard main method

```
class Round
{
        public static void main ( String[] args ) {          }
}
```

2. Inside the main method, declare and initialize a **float** variable

```
float num = 7.25f ;
```

3. Output the rounded **float** value as an **int** value

```
System.out.println( num+" rounded is "+Math.round( num ) ) ;
```

4. Output the rounded **float** value as **double** values

```
System.out.println( num+" floored is " +Math.floor( num ) );
System.out.println( num+" ceiling is " + Math.ceil( num ) ) ;
```

5. Save the program as **Round.java** then compile and run the program to see the output

By default, **Math.round()** will round up – so 7.5 would be rounded up to 8.

```
Command Prompt
C:\MyJava> javac Round.java

C:\MyJava> java Round
7.25 rounded is 7
7.25 floored is 7.0
7.25 ceiling is 8.0

C:\MyJava>
```

The **Math** class within the **java.lang** package provides two methods to compare two numerical values. The **Math.max()** method and the **Math.min()** method each require two numbers to be stated as their arguments. **Math.max()** will return the greater number and **Math.min()** will return the smaller number.

The numbers to be compared can be of any numerical data type, but the result will be returned as a **double** data type.

Compare.java

1. Start a new program named "Compare" containing the standard main method

```
class Compare
{
        public static void main ( String[] args ) {          }
}
```

2. Inside the main method, declare and initialize a **float** variable and an **int** variable

```
float num1 = 24.75f ;
int num2 = 25 ;
```

3. Output the greater value

```
System.out.println( "Most is " + Math.max( num1, num2 ) ) ;
```

4. Output the lesser value

```
System.out.println( "Least is " + Math.min( num1, num2 ) ) ;
```

5. Save the program as **Compare.java** then compile and run the program to see the output

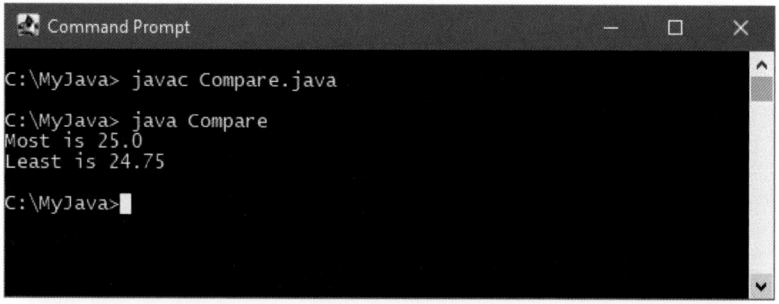

Generating random numbers

The **Math** class within the **java.lang** package provides the ability to generate random numbers with its **Math.random()** method, which returns a **double** precision random number between 0.0 and 0.999. Multiplying the random number will specify a wider range. For example, multiplying by 10 will create a random number in the range of 0.0 to 9.999. Now, rounding the random number up with **Math.ceil()** will ensure it falls within the range of 1-10 inclusive.

Random.java

1. Start a new program named "Random" containing the standard main method

```
class Random
{
        public static void main ( String[] args ) {          }
}
```

2. Inside the main method, assign a random number to a **float** variable, and output its value

```
float random = (float) Math.random() ;
System.out.println( "Random number: " + random ) ;
```

3. Assign a multiplication of the random number to a second **float** variable, and output its value

```
float multiplied = random * 10 ;
System.out.println( "Multiplied number: " + multiplied ) ;
```

4. Assign a rounded integer of the multiplied random number to an **int** variable, and output its value

```
int randomInt = (int) Math.ceil( multiplied ) ;
System.out.println( "Random Integer: " + randomInt ) ;
```

5. Save the program as **Random.java** then compile and run the program to see the output

The Lottery program described opposite combines all three steps from this example into a single statement.

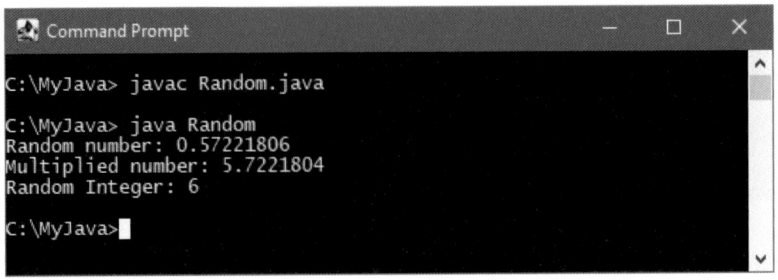

A sequence of six non-repeating random numbers within the range 1-59 inclusive can be generated using **Math.random()** to produce a random lottery selection.

Lottery.java

1. Start a new program named "Lottery" containing the standard main method

```
class Lottery
{
        public static void main ( String[] args ) {          }
}
```

2. Inside the main method, create an **int** array of 60 elements, then fill elements 1-59 with integers 1-59

```
int[] nums = new int[60] ;
for( int i = 1 ; i < 60 ; i++ ) { nums[i] = i ; }
```

3. Shuffle the values in elements 1-59

```
for( int i = 1 ; i < 60 ; i++ )
{
        int r = (int) Math.ceil( Math.random() * 59 ) ;
        int temp = nums[i] ;
        nums[i] = nums[r] ;
        nums[r] = temp ;
}
```

4. Output only those values contained in elements 1-6

```
for ( int i = 1 ; i < 7 ; i++ )
{
        System.out.print( Integer.toString( nums[i]) + " " ) ;
}
```

5. Save the program as **Lottery.java** then compile it and run the program three times to see three different sequences

This program is revisited with a graphical user interface in Chapter 10.

```
Command Prompt
C:\MyJava> javac Lottery.java

C:\MyJava> java Lottery
37  41  9  39  27  53
C:\MyJava> java Lottery
54  47  5  19  20  38
C:\MyJava> java Lottery
10  34  44  39  51  33
C:\MyJava>
```

Managing strings

In Java programming, a **String** is zero or more characters enclosed within quotation marks. So, these are all valid **String** values:

```
String txt1 = "My First String" ;

String txt2 = "" ;

String txt3 = "2" ;

String txt4 = "null" ;
```

The empty quotes of **txt2** initialize the variable as an empty **String** value. The numeric value assigned to **txt3** is a **String** representation of the number. The Java **null** keyword, which normally represents the absence of any value, is simply a **String** literal when it is enclosed within quotes.

Essentially, a **String** is a collection of characters; each character containing its own data – just like elements in a defined array. It is, therefore, logical to regard a **String** as an array of characters and apply array characteristics when dealing with **String** values.

Array.length is a property but **String.length()** is a method – so it must have trailing parentheses.

The **String** class is part of the fundamental **java.lang** package and provides a **length()** method that will return the size of a **String**, much like the **length** property of an array. Each **String** variable is created as an "instance" of the **String** class so its methods can be used by tacking their name onto the variable name using dot notation. For example, the syntax to return the size of a **String** variable named **txt** is **txt.length()**.

The **String** class within the **java.lang** package also provides an alternative to the **+** concatenation operator for joining **String** values together. Its **concat()** method requires a single argument specifying the second **String** to be appended. In use it is tacked onto the variable name of the first **String** using dot notation. For example, append **txt2** onto **txt1** using **txt1.concat(txt2)**.

1. Start a new program named "StringLength" containing the standard main method

```
class StringLength
{
        public static void main ( String[] args ) {          }
}
```

StringLength.java

2. Inside the main method, create and initialize two **String** variables

```
String lang = "Java" ;
String series = " in easy steps" ;
```

3. Add another **String** variable and assign it the concatenated value of the other two **String** variables

```
String title = lang.concat( series ) ;
```

4. Output the concatenated **String** within quotation marks, together with its size

```
System.out.print( "\"" + title + "\" has " ) ;
System.out.println( title.length() + " characters" ) ;
```

5. Save the program as **StringLength.java** then compile and run the program to see the output

```
Command Prompt
C:\MyJava> javac StringLength.java

C:\MyJava> java StringLength
"Java in easy steps" has 18 characters

C:\MyJava>
```

Spaces are part of the **String** so are included in the character count – but the quotation marks are not included.

Comparing strings

The **String** class within the **java.lang** package provides the useful **equals()** method that was introduced on page 66 to evaluate a command line argument in the **args[0]** element. This can also be used to compare any two **String** values by tacking the method name onto the first **String** variable using dot notation, and specifying the **String** to be compared as its argument. For example, the syntax to compare **txt2** to **txt1** is **txt1.equals(txt2)**. When both **String** values have identical characters, in the same order, the method returns **true** – otherwise, it returns **false**.

Be sure to observe correct capitalization using a capital "C" in the toUpperCase and toLowerCase methods.

String values that use different letter case, such as "Java" and "JAVA", are not considered equal because the ASCII code values of the characters differ. For instance, the value of uppercase "A" is 65, whereas lowercase "a" is 97.

To compare an input **String** value, where the letter case entered by the user is uncertain, against a **String** value in the program it is often useful to transform the input into a particular case. For this purpose, the **String** class provides a **toUpperCase()** method and a **toLowerCase()** method. The input **String** is specified as the argument, and the method returns the transformed **String**.

A typical example might force a user-input password **String** to lowercase before comparing it to the correct password stored in all lowercase in a **String** variable within the program. This would allow the user to enter their password in uppercase, lowercase, or a mixture of both cases where case-insensitive passwords are permissible.

Dot notation allows methods to be tacked onto other methods so their operations can be performed in sequence. This means that **toLowerCase().equals()** can be used to transform a **String** value to lowercase and then compare that lowercase version against a specified argument.

StringComparison.java

1. Start a new program named "StringComparison" containing the standard main method

```
class StringComparison
{
        public static void main ( String[] args ) {      }
}
```

2. Inside the main method, create and initialize a **String** variable with a correct lowercase password

```
String password = "bingo" ;
```

3. Add a **try catch** statement to catch the exception that occurs when no password argument is entered

```
try {    }
catch( Exception e )
{
        System.out.println( "Password required." ) ;
}
```

4. Insert this **if else** statement into the **try** statement block to evaluate the password argument entered by the user

```
if ( args[0].toLowerCase().equals( password ) )
{
        System.out.println( "Password accepted." ) ;
}
else
{
        System.out.println( "Incorrect password." ) ;
}
```

5. Save the program as **StringComparison.java** then compile and run the program with various arguments

```
Command Prompt

C:\MyJava> javac StringComparison.java

C:\MyJava> java StringComparison
Password required.

C:\MyJava> java StringComparison BIMBO
Incorrect password.

C:\MyJava> java StringComparison BINGO
Password accepted.

C:\MyJava>
```

Searching strings

The **String** class within the **java.lang** package provides **startsWith()** and **endsWith()** methods to compare portions of a **String** value. These are especially useful to compare a number of **String** values and select those with common beginnings or common endings. When the **String** section matches the specified argument, the method returns **true** – otherwise, it returns **false**.

A portion of a **String** value can be copied by stating the position number of the first character to be copied as the argument to its **substring()** method. This will return a substring of the original **String** value, starting at the specified start position and ending at the end of the original **String**.

Optionally, the **substring()** method can take a second argument to specify the position number of the final character to be copied. This will return a substring of the original **String** value, starting at the specified start position and ending at the specified end position.

A **String** value can be searched to find a character or substring specified as the argument to its **indexOf()** method. Unusually, this method returns the numeric position of the first occurrence of the matched character or substring within the searched **String** value. Where no match is found, the method returns the negative integer value of -1.

StringSearch.java

1. Start a new program named "StringSearch" containing the standard main method

```
class StringSearch
{
        public static void main ( String[] args ) {          }
}
```

2. Inside the main method, create an initialized **String** array of book titles

```
String[] books  =
{       "Java in easy steps", "XML in easy steps" ,
        "SQL in easy steps" , "CSS in easy steps" ,
        "Gone With the Wind" , "Drop the Defense" } ;
```

3. Create and initialize three **int** counter variables

```
int counter1 = 0 , counter2 = 0 , counter3 = 0 ;
```

4. Add a **for** loop to iterate through the **String** array, listing as output the first four characters of each title

```
for ( int i = 0 ; i < books.length ; i++ )
{
        System.out.print( books[i].substring( 0,4 ) + " | " ) ;
}
```

5. Insert a statement in the **for** loop block to count the titles found with a specified ending

```
if ( books[i].endsWith( "in easy steps" ) ) counter1++ ;
```

6. Insert a statement in the **for** loop block to count the titles found with a specified beginning

```
if ( books[i].startsWith( "Java" ) ) counter2++ ;
```

7. Insert a statement in the **for** loop block to count the titles found not containing a specified substring

```
if ( books[i].indexOf( "easy" ) == -1 ) counter3++ ;
```

8. At the end of the main method, add these statements to output the results of each search

```
System.out.println( "\nFound " + counter1 +
                                " titles from this series" ) ;
System.out.println( "Found " + counter2 + " Java title" ) ;
System.out.println( "Found " + counter3 + " other titles" ) ;
```

9. Save the program as **StringSearch.java** then compile and run the program to see the output

```
Command Prompt

C:\MyJava> javac StringSearch.java

C:\MyJava> java StringSearch
Java | XML  | SQL  | CSS  | Gone | Drop |
Found 4 titles from this series
Found 1 Java title
Found 2 other titles

C:\MyJava>
```

The **!** NOT operator cannot be used to test if the **indexOf()** method has failed – because it returns an integer value, not a Boolean value.

Manipulating characters

The **String** class within the **java.lang** package provides the **trim()** method that is used to remove any whitespace from the beginning and end of the **String** specified as its argument. This method will remove all extreme spaces, newlines, and tabs, returning the trimmed version of that **String**.

An individual character in a **String** can be addressed by stating its index position within that **String** as the argument to its **charAt()** method. This method treats the **String** as an array of characters where the first character is at position zero – just like other arrays whose elements are indexed starting at zero. The first character in a **String** can be addressed as **charAt(0)**, the second character as **charAt(1)**, and so on.

As character indexing begins at zero, the final character in a **String** will always have an index number that is one less than the total number of characters in the **String**. This means that the final character in any **String** has the index number equivalent to **length() - 1**. The final character in a **String** named "str" can, therefore, be addressed as **str.charAt(str.length() - 1)**.

All occurrences of a particular character in a **String** can be replaced by another character using its **replace()** method. This method requires two arguments that specify the character to be replaced and the character that is to take its place. For example, to replace all occurrences of the letter "a" with the letter "z", the syntax would be **replace('a' , 'z')**.

The **isEmpty()** method can be used to discover if a **String** contains no characters. This method will return **true** if the **String** is absolutely empty, otherwise it will return **false**.

CharacterSwap.java

1. Start a new program named "CharacterSwap" containing the standard main method

```
class CharacterSwap
{
        public static void main ( String[] args ) {          }
}
```

2. Inside the main method, declare and initialize an empty **String** variable

```
String txt = "" ;
```

3. Assign some characters to the **String** variable, if it is indeed empty, with both leading and trailing spaces

```
if ( txt.isEmpty() ) txt = "     Borrocudo     " ;
```

4. Output the **String** value and the number of characters it contains

```
System.out.println( "String:  " + txt ) ;
System.out.println( "Original String Length:  " + txt.length() ) ;
```

5. Remove the leading and trailing spaces, then output the **String** value and its size again

```
txt = txt.trim() ;
System.out.println( "String: " + txt ) ;
System.out.println( "String Length:  " + txt.length() ) ;
```

6. Output the first character in the **String**

```
char initial = txt.charAt(0) ;
System.out.println( "First Letter: " + initial ) ;
```

7. Now, output the last character in the **String**

```
initial = txt.charAt( ( txt.length() -1 ) );
System.out.println( "Last Letter: " + initial ) ;
```

8. Replace all occurrences of the letter "o" with letter "a"

```
txt = txt.replace( 'o' , 'a' ) ;
System.out.println( "String: " + txt ) ;
```

9. Save the program as **CharacterSwap.java** then compile and run the program to see the output

```
Command Prompt

C:\MyJava> javac CharacterSwap.java

C:\MyJava> java CharacterSwap
String:      Borrocudo
String Length:  19
String: Borrocudo
String Length:  9
First Letter: B
Last Letter: o
String: Barracuda

C:\MyJava>
```

Summary

- The Java documentation provides information about the methods and properties in each Java class.
- Java classes that are fundamental to the Java language are contained in the **java.lang** package, in the **java.base** module.
- The **Math** class provides **Math.PI** and **Math.E** constants.
- **Math.pow()** raises to a specified power and **Math.sqrt()** returns the square root of a specified number.
- Numbers can be rounded to an integer value with **Math.round()**, **Math.floor()**, and **Math.ceil()**.
- Numbers can be compared with **Math.max()** and **Math.min()**.
- **Math.random()** returns a **double** precision random number between 0.0 and 0.999999999999999.
- A **String** is zero or more characters enclosed in quote marks.
- The **length()** method returns the size of its **String**, much like the **length** property of an array.
- The **concat()** method of a **String** appends another **String** value.
- The **equals()** method of a **String** only returns **true** when two **String** values have identical characters, in the same order.
- Character case of a **String** can be changed using its **toUpperCase()** method and **toLowerCase()** method.
- **String** values can be compared using the **startsWith()** and **endsWith()** methods of a **String**.
- A substring can be sought in a **String** using its **indexOf()** and **substring()** methods.
- The **isEmpty()** method only returns **true** when the **String** contains absolutely nothing.
- Characters can be manipulated within a **String** value using its **trim()**, **charAt()**, and **replace()** methods.

6 Creating classes

This chapter demonstrates how to create Java programs that employ multiple methods and classes.

98 Forming multiple methods

100 Understanding program scope

102 Forming multiple classes

104 Extending an existing class

106 Creating an object class

108 Producing an object instance

110 Encapsulating properties

112 Constructing object values

114 Summary

Forming multiple methods

Programs are typically split into separate methods in order to create modules of code that each perform tasks, and that can be called repeatedly throughout the program as required. Splitting the program into multiple methods also makes it easier to track down bugs, as each method can be tested individually. Further methods may be declared, inside the curly brackets that follow the class declaration, using the same keywords that are used to declare the main method. Each new method must be given a name, following the usual naming conventions, and may optionally specify arguments in the parentheses after its name.

Methods.java

1. Start a new program named "Methods" containing the standard main method

```
class Methods
{
        public static void main ( String[] args ) {          }
}
```

2. Between the curly brackets of the main method, insert statements to output a message and to call a second method named "sub"

```
System.out.println( "Message from the main method." ) ;
sub() ;
```

3. After the main method, before the final curly bracket of the class, add the second method to output a message

```
public static void sub()
{
   System.out.println( "Message from the sub method." ) ;
}
```

4. Save the program as **Methods.java** then compile and run the program to see the output

The syntax to call a method without arguments just needs the method name, followed by parentheses.

A class may even contain multiple methods of the same name providing they each have different arguments – requiring a different number of arguments, or arguments of different data types. This useful feature is known as method "overloading".

Overload.java

1. Start a new program named "Overload" containing the standard main method

```
class Overload
{
        public static void main ( String[] args ) {          }
}
```

2. Between the curly brackets of the main method, insert three statements calling different overloaded methods and passing them argument values

```
System.out.println( write( 12 ) ) ;
System.out.println( write( "Twelve" ) ) ;
System.out.println( write( 4 , 16 ) ) ;
```

3. After the main method, before the final curly bracket of the class, add the three overloaded methods to each return a **String** to the caller

```
public static String write( int num )
{       return ( "Integer passed is " + num ) ;   }

public static String write( String num )
{       return ( "String passed is " + num ) ;    }

public static String write( int num1 , int num2 )
{       return ( "Sum Total is " + ( num1 * num2 ) ) ;    }
```

4. Save the program as **Overload.java** then compile and run the program to see the output

The declaration for each of the overloaded methods must indicate that the method returns a **String** value, not **void**.

```
Command Prompt

C:\MyJava> javac Overload.java

C:\MyJava> java Overload
Integer passed is 12
String passed is Twelve
Sum Total is 64

C:\MyJava>
```

Understanding program scope

A variable that is declared inside a method is only accessible from inside that method – its "scope" of accessibility is only local to the method in which it is declared. This means that a variable of the same name can be declared in another method without conflict.

Scope.java

1. Start a new program named "Scope" containing the standard main method

```
class Scope
{
        public static void main ( String[] args ) {        }
}
```

2. Between the curly brackets of the main method declare and initialize a local **String** variable, then output its value

```
String txt = "This is a local variable in the main method" ;
System.out.println( txt ) ;
```

3. After the main method, before the final curly bracket of the class, add another method named "sub"

```
public static void sub( ) {        }
```

4. Between the curly brackets of the sub method, declare and initialize a local **String** variable of the same name as the variable in the main method

```
String txt = "This is a local variable in the sub method" ;
System.out.println( txt ) ;
```

5. Insert a call to the sub method at the end of the main method

```
sub() ;
```

6. Save the program as **Scope.java** then compile and run the program to see the output

A counter variable declared in a **for** loop cannot be accessed outside the loop – its scope is limited to the **for** statement block.

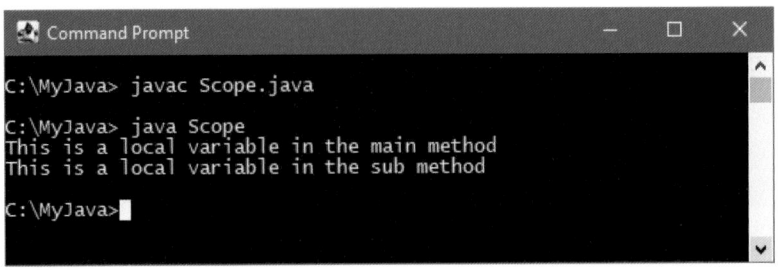

The **static** keyword that is used in method declarations ensures that the method is a "class method" – globally accessible from any other method in the class.

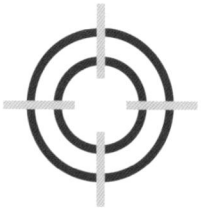

Similarly, a "class variable" can be declared with the **static** keyword to ensure it is globally accessible throughout the class. Its declaration should be made before the main method declaration, right after the curly bracket following the class declaration.

A program may have a global class variable and local method variable of the same name. The local method variable takes precedence unless the global class variable is explicitly addressed by the class name prefix using dot notation, or if a local variable of that name has not been declared.

7. Edit **Scope.java** by inserting a global class **String** variable constant of the same name as the local method variables
```
final static String txt =
        "This is a global variable of the Scope class" ;
```

8. Add a statement at the end of the main method to output the value of the global class variable
```
System.out.println( Scope.txt ) ;
```

9. Comment out the line that declares the local variable in the sub method – so the output statement will now address the global variable of the same name
```
//String txt = "This is a local variable in the sub method" ;
```

10. Save the changes, then recompile the program and run it once more to see the revised output

```
Command Prompt

C:\MyJava> javac Scope.java

C:\MyJava> java Scope
This is a local variable in the main method
This is a global variable of the Scope class
This is a global variable of the Scope class

C:\MyJava>
```

Use local method variables wherever possible to avoid conflicts – global class variables are typically only used for constants.

Forming multiple classes

In the same way that a program may have multiple methods, larger programs may consist of several classes – where each class provides specific functionality. This modular format is generally preferable to writing the entire program in a single class, as it makes debugging easier and provides better flexibility.

The **public** keyword that appears in declarations is an "access modifier" that determines how visible an item will be to other classes. It can be used in the class declaration to explicitly ensure that class will be visible to any other class. If it is omitted, the default access control level allows access from other local classes. The **public** keyword must always be used with the program's main method, however, so that method will be visible to the compiler.

Multi.java

1. Start a new program named "Multi" containing the standard main method – including the **public** keyword as usual

```
class Multi
{
        public static void main ( String[] args ) {          }
}
```

2. Between the curly brackets of the main method, declare and initialize a **String** variable, then output its contents

```
String msg = "This is a local variable in the Multi class" ;
System.out.println( msg ) ;
```

3. Output the contents of a class **String** variable constant named "txt" from a class named "Data"

```
System.out.println( Data.txt ) ;
```

4. Call a method named "greeting" from the Data class

```
Data.greeting() ;
```

5. Call a method named "line" from a class named "Draw"

```
Draw.line() ;
```

6. Save the program as **Multi.java**

The compiler will automatically find classes in adjacent external **.java** files – and create compiled **.class** files for each one.

7. Start a new file creating the Data class

```
class Data
{

}
```

Data.java

8. Declare and initialize a public class variable constant

```
public final static String txt =
        "This is a global variable in the Data class" ;
```

9. Add a public "greeting" class method

```
public static void greeting()
{
        System.out.print( "This is a global method " ) ;
        System.out.println( "of the Data class" ) ;
}
```

10. Save the file as **Data.java** in the same directory as the **Multi.java** program

11. Start a new file creating a Draw class and a class "line" method for default access – without the **public** keyword

```
class Draw
{
  static void line()
  {
        System.out.println( "_________________________" ) ;
  }
}
```

Draw.java

12. Save the file as **Draw.java** in the same directory as the **Multi.java** program, then compile and run the program to see the output

```
C:\MyJava> javac Multi.java

C:\MyJava> java Multi
This is a local variable in the Multi class
This is a global variable of the Data class
This is a global method of the Data class
_____________________________________

C:\MyJava>
```

The **public** keyword allows access from any other class, but default access only allows access from classes in the same package.

Extending an existing class

A class can inherit the features of another class by using the **extends** keyword in the class declaration to specify the name of the class from which it should inherit. For example, the declaration **class Extra extends Base** inherits from the **Base** class.

The inheriting class is described as the "sub" class, and the class from which it inherits is described as the "super" class. In the example declaration above, the **Base** class is the super class and the **Extra** class is the sub class.

Methods and variables created in a super class can generally be treated as if they existed in the sub class providing they have not been declared with the **private** keyword, which denies access from outside the original class.

A method in a sub class will override a method of the same name that exists in its super class unless their arguments differ. The method in the super class may be explicitly addressed using its class name and dot notation – for example, **SuperClass.run()**.

It should be noted that a **try catch** statement in a method within a super class does not catch exceptions that occur in a sub class – the calling statement must be enclosed within its own **try catch** statement to catch those exceptions.

SuperClass.java

1. Start a new class named "SuperClass"

```
class SuperClass {        }
```

2. Between the curly brackets of the class, add a method that outputs an identifying **String**

```
public static void hello( )
{
        System.out.println( "Hello from the Super Class" ) ;
}
```

3. Add a second method that attempts to output a passed argument, then save the file as **SuperClass.java**

```
public static void echo( String arg )
{
        try
        { System.out.println( "You entered: " + arg ) ;    }
        catch( Exception e )
        { System.out.println( "Argument required" ) ;      }
}
```

4. Start a new program named "SubClass" that extends the SuperClass class

```
class SubClass extends SuperClass
{
        public static void main ( String[] args ) {          }
}
```

SubClass.java

5. After the main method, add a method that outputs an identifying **String**, overriding the inherited method of the same name

```
public static void hello()
{
        System.out.println( "Hello from the Sub Class" ) ;
}
```

6. Between the curly brackets of the main method, insert a call to the overriding method and then explicitly call the method of the same name in the super class

```
hello() ;
SuperClass.hello() ;
```

7. Add a call to the other inherited method

```
echo( args[0] ) ;
```

8. Save the program as **SubClass.java** then compile and run the program without a command line argument

```
Command Prompt

C:\MyJava> javac SubClass.java

C:\MyJava> java SubClass
Hello from the Sub Class
Hello from the Super Class
Exception in thread "main" java.lang.ArrayIndexOutOfBoundsException:
Index 0 out of bounds for length 0
        at SubClass.main(SubClass.java:9)

C:\MyJava>
```

9. Edit **SubClass.java** to enclose the method call in Step 7, to place it within its own **try catch** statement to catch exceptions, then recompile and re-run the program to see the problem resolved

You can find more information about catching exceptions on page 76.

Creating an object class

Real-world objects are all around us, and they each have attributes and behaviors that we can describe:

- Attributes describe the features that an object has.
- Behaviors describe actions that an object can perform.

For example, a car might be described with attributes of "red" and "coupe", along with an "accelerate" behavior.

These features could be represented in Java programming with a **Car** class containing variable properties of **color** and **bodyType**, along with an **accelerate()** method.

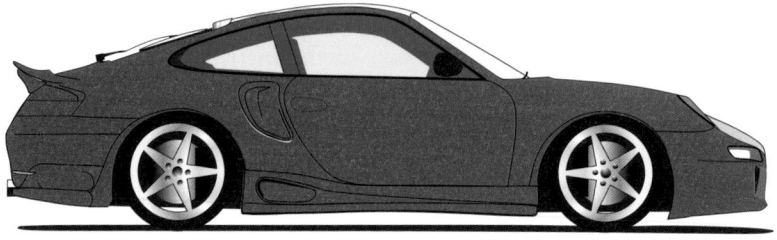

Java is said to be an Object Oriented Programming (OOP) language because it makes extensive use of object attributes and behaviors to perform program tasks.

Objects are created in Java by defining a class as a template from which different copies, or "instances", can be made.

Each instance of the class can be customized by assigning attribute values and behaviors to describe that object.

The **Car** class is created as a class template in the steps described opposite – with the default attributes and behavior outlined above. An instance of the **Car** class is created in the steps described on page 109, inheriting the same default attributes and behavior.

1. Start a new template class named "Car"

```
class Car
{

}
```

FirstObject.java

2. Between the curly brackets of the **Car** class, declare and initialize two global **String** constants describing attributes

```
public final static String color = "Red" ;
public final static String bodyType = "Coupe" ;
```

3. Add a global method describing a behavior

```
public static String accelerate()
{
        String motion = "Accelerating -->" ;
        return motion ;
}
```

The **static** keyword declares class variables and class methods – in this case, as members of the **Car** class.

4. After the **Car** class, start a new program class named "FirstObject" containing the standard main method

```
class FirstObject
{
        public static void main ( String[] args ) {          }
}
```

5. Between the curly brackets of the main method, insert statements to output the value of each **Car** attribute and call its behavior method

```
System.out.println( "Paint is " + Car.color ) ;
System.out.println( "Style is " + Car.bodyType ) ;
System.out.println( Car.accelerate() ) ;
```

Object classes are normally created before the program class containing the main method.

6. Save the program as **FirstObject.java** then compile and run the program to see the output

```
Command Prompt
C:\MyJava> javac FirstObject.java

C:\MyJava> java FirstObject
Paint is Red
Style is Coupe
Accelerating -->

C:\MyJava>
```

Producing an object instance

Each class has a built-in "constructor" method that can be used to create a new instance of that class. The constructor method has the same name as the class, and is invoked with the **new** keyword.

Each instance of a class inherits the object's attributes and behaviors. The principle of inheritance is used throughout Java so that programs can use ready-made properties.

To be more flexible, object class templates can be defined in a file other than that containing the program. This means they can be readily used by multiple programs.

Car.java

1. Start a new file, repeating the **Car** class object template from the previous example on pages 106-107

```
class Car
{
        public final static String color = "Red" ;
        public final static String bodyType = "Coupe" ;
        public static String accelerate()
        {
                String motion = "Accelerating -->" ;
                return motion ;
        }
}
```

2. Save the file as **Car.java**

FirstInstance.java

3. Start a new program named "FirstInstance" containing the standard main method

```
class FirstInstance
{
        public static void main ( String[] args ) {          }
}
```

4. Between the curly brackets of the main method, insert statements to output the value of each attribute of the **Car** class and call its behavior method

```
System.out.println( "Car paint is " + Car.color ) ;
System.out.println( "Car style is "+ Car.bodyType ) ;
System.out.println( Car.accelerate() ) ;
```

5. Now, add a statement to create a **Porsche** instance of the **Car** class
```
Car Porsche = new Car() ;
```

6. Add statements to output the inherited value of each **Porsche** attribute and call its behavior method
```
System.out.println( "Porsche paint is " + Porsche.color ) ;
System.out.println( "Porsche style is " + Porsche.bodyType ) ;
System.out.println( Porsche.accelerate() ) ;
```

7. Save the program as **FirstInstance.java** alongside the **Car.java** template file, then compile and run the program to see the output

You cannot address the **motion** variable directly – it is out of scope within the method declaration.

```
Command Prompt

C:\MyJava> javac FirstInstance.java

C:\MyJava> java FirstInstance
Car paint is Red
Car style is Coupe
Accelerating -->
Porsche paint is Red
Porsche style is Coupe
Accelerating -->

C:\MyJava>
```

A virtual class is created for the new **Porsche** object that replicates the original **Car** class. Both these objects contain static "class variables" and a "class method", which are addressed using the class name and dot notation – as these members are globally accessible, this is not considered good programming practice.

Whilst this example demonstrates how instances of an object inherit properties of the original class, it is improved in the next example on pages 110-111 that uses non-static members to create "instance variables" and an "instance method", which cannot be addressed from outside that class – as these members are not globally accessible, this is considered good programming practice.

The compiler automatically finds the **Car** class in the external **.java** file – and creates a compiled **.class** file for it.

Encapsulating properties

The **private** keyword can be used when declaring object variables and methods to protect them from manipulation by external program code. The object should then include **public** methods to retrieve the values and call the methods. This technique neatly encapsulates the variables and methods within the object structure. It is demonstrated in the following steps that reproduce the previous example – but with encapsulated attributes and method:

SafeInstance.java

1. Start a new class named "Car"

```
class Car
{

}
```

2. Between the curly brackets of the class, declare three private **String** variables to store object attributes

```
private String maker ;
private String color ;
private String bodyType ;
```

3. Add a private method describing a behavior

```
private String accelerate()
{
        String motion = "Accelerating -->" ;
        return motion ;
}
```

4. Add a public method to assign passed argument values to each private variable

```
public void setCar( String brand , String paint , String style )
{
        maker = brand ;
        color = paint ;
        bodyType = style ;
}
```

5. Add another public method to retrieve the private variable values and to call the private method

```
public void getCar()
{
  System.out.println( maker + " paint is " + color ) ;
  System.out.println( maker + " style is " + bodyType ) ;
  System.out.println( maker + " is " + accelerate() + "\n" ) ;
}
```

6. After the end of the **Car** class, start another class named "SafeInstance" containing the standard main method

```
class SafeInstance
{
        public static void main ( String[] args) {          }
}
```

7. Between the curly brackets of the main method, insert a statement to create an instance of the **Car** class

```
Car Porsche = new Car() ;
```

8. Add a statement that calls a public method of the **Car** class to assign values to its private variables

```
Porsche.setCar( "Porsche" , "Red" , "Coupe" ) ;
```

9. Now, add a statement to call the other public method of the **Car** class to retrieve the stored attribute values and call the private behavior method

```
Porsche.getCar() ;
```

10. Create another instance, assigning and retrieving values

```
Car Bentley = new Car() ;
Bentley.setCar( "Bentley" , "Green" , "Saloon" ) ;
Bentley.getCar() ;
```

11. Save the program as **SafeInstance.java** then compile and run the program to see the output

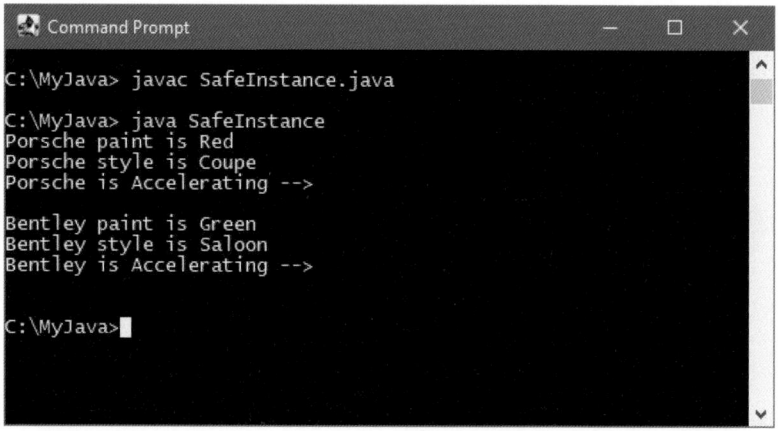

An uninitialized **String** variable has a **null** value – so calling the **getCar()** method before **setCar()** will return a **null** from each variable.

Constructing object values

An object's constructor method can be called directly in the object class to initialize object variables. This helps to keep the declarations and assignments separate, and is considered to be good programming style. It is demonstrated in the following steps that reproduce the previous example on pages 110-111 with encapsulated attributes and method – together with initialization by the constructor:

Constructor.java

1. Start a new class named "Car"

```
class Car
{

}
```

2. Between the curly brackets of the class, declare three private **String** variables to store object attributes

```
private String maker ;
private String color ;
private String bodyType ;
```

3. Add a constructor method that initializes all three variables with attribute values

```
public Car()
{
        maker = "Porsche" ;
        color = "Silver" ;
        bodyType = "Coupe" ;
}
```

Constructor method declarations do not state any return data type.

4. Add a private method describing a behavior

```
private String accelerate()
{
        String motion = "Accelerating -->" ;
        return motion ;
}
```

5. Add a public method to assign passed argument values to each private variable

```
public void setCar( String brand , String paint , String style )
{
        maker = brand ;
        color = paint ;
        bodyType = style ;
}
```

6. Add another public method to retrieve the private variable values and to call the private method

```
public void getCar()
{
  System.out.println( maker + " paint is " + color ) ;
  System.out.println( maker + " style is " + bodyType ) ;
  System.out.println( maker + " is " + accelerate() + "\n" ) ;
}
```

7. After the end of the **Car** class, start another class named "Constructor" containing the standard main method

```
class Constructor
{
        public static void main ( String[] args ) {          }
}
```

8. Between the curly brackets of the main method, insert statements to create an instance of the **Car** class and retrieve the initial default values

```
Car Porsche = new Car() ;
Porsche.getCar() ;
```

9. Create another instance, assigning and retrieving values

```
Car Ferrari = new Car() ;
Ferrari.setCar( "Ferrari" , "Red" , "Sport" ) ;
Ferrari.getCar() ;
```

10. Save the program as **Constructor.java** then compile and run the program to see the output

```
Command Prompt

C:\MyJava> javac Constructor.java

C:\MyJava> java Constructor
Porsche paint is Silver
Porsche style is Coupe
Porsche is Accelerating -->

Ferrari paint is Red
Ferrari style is Sport
Ferrari is Accelerating -->

C:\MyJava>
```

Summary

- Splitting programs into multiple methods, which can be called upon when required, increases flexibility and makes it easier to track down bugs.
- Overloaded methods have the same name but take different arguments.
- Variables declared within a method have local scope, but class variables have global scope throughout that class.
- The **static** keyword is used to declare class methods and class variables – having global scope throughout that class.
- The **public** keyword explicitly allows access from any class.
- A class declaration can include the **extends** keyword to nominate a super class from which it will inherit.
- The class name and dot notation can be used to explicitly address a particular class method or class variable.
- Real-world objects have attributes and behaviors that can be represented in programs by variables and methods.
- Java objects are created as a template class from which instance copies can be made.
- Each class has a constructor method that can be invoked using the **new** keyword to create an instance copy of that class.
- Instances inherit the attributes and behaviors of the class from which they are derived.
- Encapsulation protects instance variables and instance methods from manipulation by external classes.
- The **private** keyword denies access from outside the class where the declaration is made.
- An object's constructor method can be called to initialize variable attributes of that object.

7 Importing functions

This chapter demonstrates how to import additional program functionality from specialized Java classes.

116 Handling files

118 Reading console input

120 Reading files

122 Writing files

124 Sorting array elements

126 Making array lists

128 Managing dates

130 Formatting numbers

132 Summary

Handling files

Java contains a package named **java.io** that is designed to handle file input and output procedures. The package can be made available to a program by including an **import** statement at the very beginning of the **.java** file. This can use the * wildcard character to mean "all classes" in the statement **import java.io.* ;** .

The **java.io** package has a class named "File" that can be used to access files or complete directories. A **File** object must first be created using the **new** keyword and specifying the filename, or directory name, as the constructor's argument. For example, the syntax to create a **File** object named "info" to represent a local file named "info.dat" looks like this:

```
File info = new File( "info.dat" ) ;
```

This file would be located in the same directory as the program, but the argument could state the path to a file located elsewhere. Note that the creation of a **File** object does not actually create a file, but merely the means to represent a file.

Once a **File** object has been created to represent a file, its methods can be called to manipulate the file. The most useful **File** object methods are listed in this table, together with a brief description:

Method:	Returns:
exists()	**true** if the file exists – **false** if it does not
getName()	the filename as a **String**
length()	number of bytes in the file, as a **long** type
createNewFile()	**true** if able to create the new unique file
delete()	**true** if able to successfully delete the file
renameTo(File)	**true** if able to successfully rename the file
list()	an array of file or folder names as **Strings**

The filename specified as the constructor argument must be enclosed within quotes.

ListFiles.java

1. Start a new program that imports the functionality of all the **java.io** classes
```
import java.io.* ;
```

2. Add a class named "ListFiles" containing the standard main method
```
class ListFiles
{
        public static void main( String[] args ) {          }
}
```

3. Between the curly brackets of the main method, insert a statement to create a **File** object for a directory folder named "data"
```
File dir = new File( "data" ) ;
```

4. Add an **if** statement to output the names of all files in that folder, or a message if the folder is empty
```
if ( dir.exists() )
{
        String[] files = dir.list() ;
        System.out.println( files.length + " files found..." ) ;
        for ( int i = 0 ; i < files.length ; i++ )
        {
                System.out.println( files[i] ) ;
        }
}
else
{       System.out.println( "Folder not found." ) ;         }
```

5. Save the program as **ListFiles.java** alongside a "data" folder containing some files, then compile and run the program to see the filenames listed as output

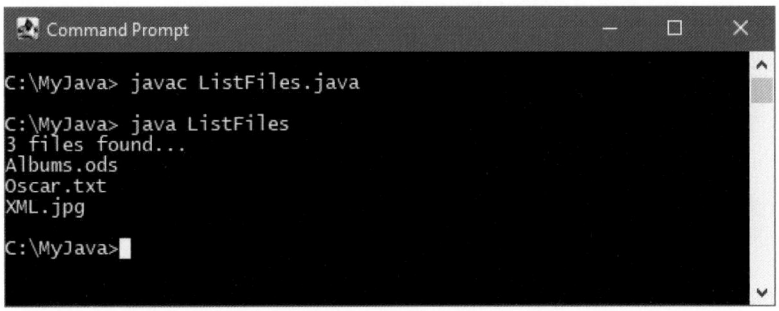

Reading console input

The **java.io** package allows a program to read input from the command line – interacting with the user. Just as the **System.out** field can send output to the command line, the **System.in** field can be used to read from it with an **InputStreamReader** object. This reads the input as bytes, which it converts into integer values that represent Unicode character values.

In order to read an entire line of input text, the **readLine()** method of a **BufferedReader** object reads the characters decoded by the **InputStreamReader.** This method must be called from within a **try catch** statement to catch any **IOException** problems.

Typically, the **readLine()** method will assign the input to a **String** variable for manipulation by the program.

ReadString.java

1. Start a new program that imports the functionality of all the **java.io** classes
```
import java.io.* ;
```

2. Add a class named "ReadString" containing the standard main method
```
class ReadString
{
        public static void main( String[] args ) {          }
}
```

3. Between the curly brackets of the main method, insert a statement to output a message prompting the user for input
```
System.out.print( "Enter the title of this book: " ) ;
```

4. Add a statement creating an **InputStreamReader** object, enabling input to be read from the command line
```
InputStreamReader isr =
                new InputStreamReader( System.in ) ;
```

5. Create a **BufferedReader** object to read the decoded input
```
BufferedReader buffer = new BufferedReader( isr ) ;
```

6. Declare and initialize an empty **String** variable in which to store the input
```
String input = "" ;
```

7. Add a **try catch** statement to read the input from the command line and store it in the variable

```
try
{
        input = buffer.readLine() ;
        buffer.close() ;
}
catch ( IOException e )
{
        System.out.println( "An input error has occurred" ) ;
}
```

8. Output a message that includes the stored value

```
System.out.println( "\nThanks, you are reading " + input ) ;
```

9. Save the program as **ReadString.java** then compile and run the program

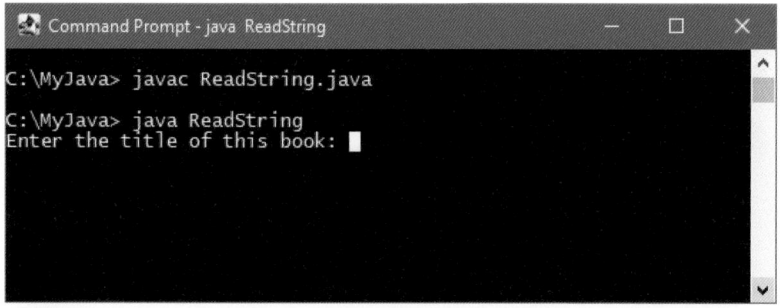

10. Enter text as prompted, then hit Return to see the output message containing your input text

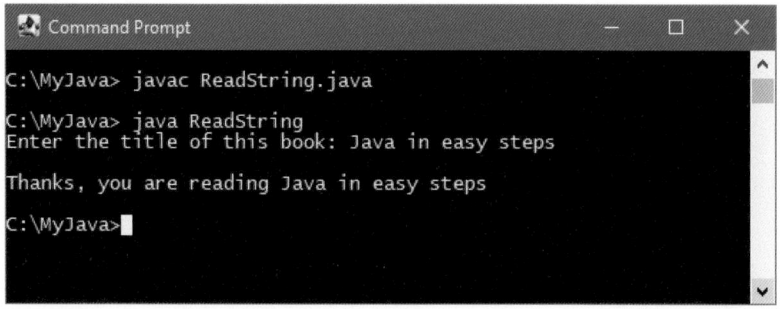

It is good practice to call the **close()** method of the **BufferedReader** object when it is no longer needed.

Reading files

The **java.io** package contains a class named **FileReader** that is especially designed to read text files. This class is a subclass of the **InputStreamReader** class that can be used to read console input by converting a byte stream into integers that represent Unicode character values.

A **FileReader** object is created using the **new** keyword, and takes the name of the file to be read as its argument. Optionally, the argument can include the full path to a file outside the directory where the program is located.

In order to efficiently read the text file line-by-line, the **readLine()** method of a **BufferedReader** object can be employed to read the characters decoded by the **FileReader** object. This method must be called from within a **try catch** statement to catch any **IOException** problems that may arise.

Reading all lines in a text file containing multiple lines of text is accomplished by making repeated calls to the **readLine()** method in a loop. At the end of the file the call will return a **null** value, which can be used to terminate the loop.

1 Open a plain text editor, such as Windows Notepad, and write a few lines of text – for example, a famous verse from "The Ballad of Reading Gaol" by Oscar Wilde

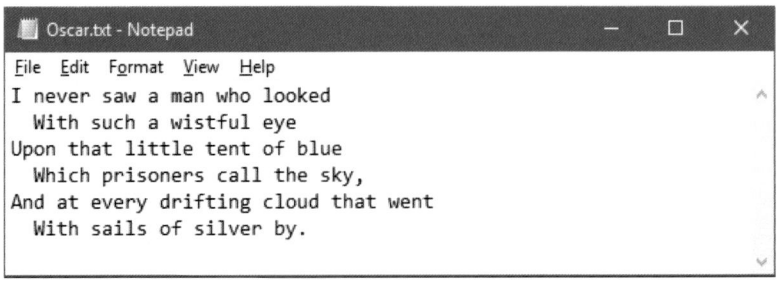

ReadFile.java

2 Save the text file as **Oscar.txt** then start a new program that imports the functionality of all the **java.io** classes
import java.io.* ;

3 Add a class named "ReadFile" containing the standard main method

```
class ReadFile
{       public static void main( String[] args ) {    }     }
```

4. Between the curly brackets of the main method, insert a **try catch** statement

```
try {     }
catch ( IOException e )
{
        System.out.println( "A read error has occurred" ) ;
}
```

5. Between the curly brackets of the **try** block, insert a statement to create a **FileReader** object

```
FileReader file = new FileReader( "Oscar.txt" ) ;
```

6. Create a **BufferedReader** object to read the file

```
BufferedReader buffer = new BufferedReader( file ) ;
```

7. Declare and initialize an empty **String** variable in which to store a line of text

```
String line = "" ;
```

8. Add a loop to read the text file contents into the variable and output each line of text

```
while ( ( line = buffer.readLine() ) != null )
{       System.out.println( line ) ;       }
```

9. Remember to close the **BufferedReader** object when it is no longer needed

```
buffer.close() ;
```

10. Save the program as **ReadFile.java** alongside the text file, then compile and run the program to see the output

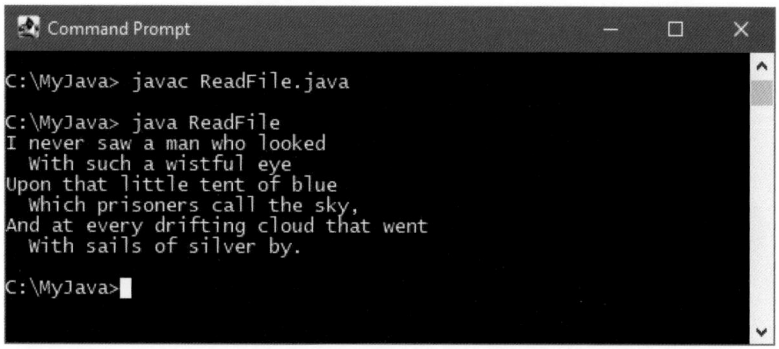

The text file specified as the **FileReader** argument must be enclosed within quotation marks.

Writing files

In the **java.io** package the **FileReader** and **BufferedReader** classes, which are used to read text files, have counterparts named **FileWriter** and **BufferedWriter** that can be used to write text files.

A **FileWriter** object is created using the **new** keyword, and takes the name of the file to be written as its argument. Optionally, the argument can include the full path to a file to be written in a directory outside that in which the program is located.

The **BufferedWriter** object is created with the **new** keyword, and takes the name of the **FileWriter** object as its argument. Text can then be written with the **write()** method of the **BufferedWriter** object, and lines separated by calling its **newLine()** method. These methods should be called from within a **try catch** statement to catch any **IOException** problems that may arise.

If a file of the specified name already exists, its contents will be overwritten by the **write()** method, otherwise a new file of that name will be created and its contents written.

WriteFile.java

1. Start a new program that imports the functionality of all the **java.io** classes

```
import java.io.* ;
```

2. Add a class named "WriteFile" containing the standard main method

```
class WriteFile
{
        public static void main ( String[] args ) {          }
}
```

3. Between the curly brackets of the main method, insert a **try catch** statement

```
try {    }
catch ( IOException e )
{
        System.out.println( "A write error has occurred" ) ;
}
```

4. Between the curly brackets of the **try** block, insert a statement to create a **FileWriter** object for a text file named "Tam.txt"

```
FileWriter file = new FileWriter( "Tam.txt" ) ;
```

5. Create a **BufferedWriter** object to write the file
```
BufferedWriter buffer = new BufferedWriter( file ) ;
```

6. Add statements to write lines of text and newline characters into the text file – for example, a translated verse from "Tam O'Shanter" by Robert Burns
```
buffer.write( "The wind blew as if it had blown its last" ) ;
        buffer.newLine() ;
buffer.write( "The rattling showers rose on its blast" ) ;
        buffer.newLine() ;
buffer.write( "The speedy gleams the darkness swallowed" ) ;
        buffer.newLine() ;
buffer.write( "Loud, deep and long the thunder bellowed" ) ;
        buffer.newLine() ;
buffer.write( "That night a child might understand" ) ;
        buffer.newLine() ;
buffer.write( "The devil had business on his hand." ) ;
```

7. Remember to close the **BufferedWriter** object when it is no longer needed
```
buffer.close() ;
```

8. Save the program as **WriteFile.java** then compile and run the program to write the text file alongside the program

```
Command Prompt
C:\MyJava> javac WriteFile.java
C:\MyJava> java WriteFile
C:\MyJava>
```

```
Tam.txt - Notepad
File  Edit  Format  View  Help
The wind blew as if it had blown its last
The rattling showers rose on its blast
The speedy gleams the darkness swallowed
Loud, deep and long the thunder bellowed
That night a child might understand
The devil had business on his hand.
```

You can call the **append()** method of the **BufferedWriter** object to add text – rather than overwriting text with the **write()** method.

Sorting array elements

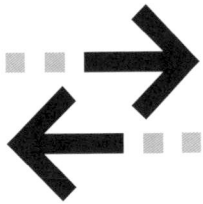

Java contains a package named **java.util** that provides useful utilities for handling collections of data. The package can be made available to a program by including an **import** statement at the very beginning of the **.java** file. This can use the * wildcard character to mean "all classes" in the statement **import java.util.* ;** .

The **java.util** package has a class named "Arrays" that has methods that can be used to manipulate arrays. Its functionality can be made available to the program by importing all classes from the **java.util** package or, where the program only requires a single class, the **import** statement can import just that specific class. For example, the program can import the **Arrays** class with the statement **import java.util.Arrays ;** .

The **Arrays** class has a **sort()** method that can rearrange the contents of array elements alphabetically and numerically.

Sort.java

1. Start a new program that imports the functionality of all methods in the **java.util.Arrays** class

```
import java.util.Arrays ;
```

2. Add a class named "Sort" containing the standard main method

```
class Sort
{       public static void main( String[] args ) { }        }
```

3. After the main method, insert a method to display all element contents of a passed **String** array

```
public static void display( String[] elems )
{
        System.out.println( "\nString Array:" ) ;
        for ( int i = 0 ; i < elems.length ; i++ )
        System.out.println( "Element "+i+" is "+elems[i] ) ;
}
```

4. Add an overloaded version of the **display()** method to display all element contents of a passed **int** array

```
public static void display( int[] elems )
{
        System.out.println( "\nInteger Array:" ) ;
        for ( int i = 0 ; i < elems.length ; i++ )
        System.out.println( "Element "+i+" is "+elems[i] ) ;
}
```

See page 99 for more on overloading methods.

5. Between the curly brackets of the main method, declare and initialize a **String** array and an **int** array
```
String[] names = { "Mike" , "Dave" , "Andy" } ;
int[] nums = { 200 , 300 , 100 } ;
```

6. Output the contents of all elements in each array
```
display( names ) ;
display( nums ) ;
```

7. Sort the element contents of both arrays
```
Arrays.sort( names ) ;
Arrays.sort( nums ) ;
```

8. Output the contents of all elements in each array again
```
display( names ) ;
display( nums ) ;
```

9. Save the program as **Sort.java** then compile and run the program to see the output

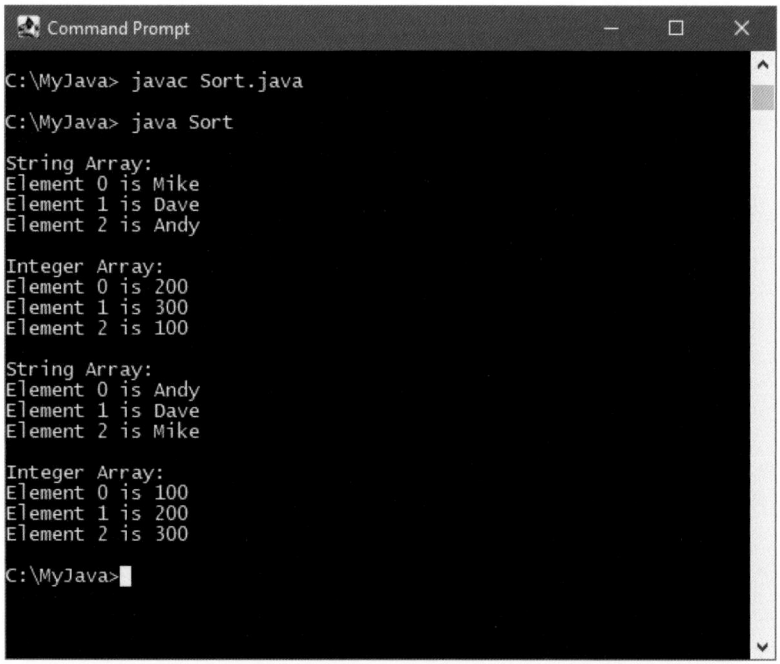

The **for** loops in this example each execute a single statement so no curly brackets are required – but they could be added for clarity.

Making array lists

The **java.util** package contains a class named **ArrayList** that stores data in an ordered "Collection" (resizable sequence) of list elements. This can be made available to a program by importing the specific class with **import java.util.ArrayList;**. A list may contain duplicate elements, and an **ArrayList** object has useful methods that allow manipulation of stored values by specifying their element index number. For example, the list's method call **get(0)** will retrieve the value stored in the first element whereas **remove(1)** will remove the second list element.

You can discover how many elements a list currently has by calling its **size()** method.

Element values can be modified by specifying the index number and new value as arguments to the list's **set()** method. Elements can be added to the list at a particular position by specifying the index number and value as arguments to the list's **add()** method. The list expands to accommodate additional elements by moving the element values along the index.

An **ArrayList** object is simply created using the **new** keyword but, like other Java collections, the statement must specify which generic type of item the list may contain. Typically, a list may contain **String** items, so **ArrayList** must have a **<String>** suffix.

Collections, such as **ArrayList**, have a **forEach()** method that iterates over each element in the list. This makes it easy to loop through all items contained in the list.

Lambda expressions were introduced in Java 8 to enable succinct anonymous methods.

Each stored list item can be conveniently referenced in turn by specifying a "lambda expression" as the argument to the **forEach()** method. Lambda expressions are simply short, anonymous (unnamed) methods that can be specified in the location they are to be executed. They begin with parentheses, to contain any arguments, then have a **->** character sequence followed by the statement block, with this syntax:

(*argument/s*) -> { *statement/s* }

The data type of the arguments can be explicitly declared, or it can be inferred from the context – **(String x)** can be simply **(x)**. Additionally, the curly brackets can be omitted if the lambda expression statement block contains only one statement.

With a list's **forEach()** method the value of the current element in the iteration can be passed to the lambda expression as its argument, then displayed in output by its statement.

1. Start a new program that imports the functionality of all methods in the **java.util.ArrayList** class
```
import java.util.ArrayList ;
```

2. Add a class named "Lists" containing the standard main method
```
class Lists
{       public static void main( String[] args ) { }        }
```

3. Between the curly brackets of the main method, insert a statement to create a **String ArrayList** object named "list"
```
ArrayList<String> list = new ArrayList<String>() ;
```

4. Next, add statements to populate the list elements with **String** values then display the entire list
```
list.add( "Alpha" ) ;
list.add( "Delta" ) ;
list.add( "Charlie" ) ;
System.out.println( "List: " + list ) ;
```

5. Now, identify the current value in the second element then replace it with a new **String**
```
System.out.println( "Replacing: " + list.get(1) + "\n" ) ;
list.set( 1, "Bravo" ) ;
```

6. Finally, iterate through the list and display the **String** value now stored in each element
```
list.forEach( ( x ) -> System.out.println( "Item: " + x ) ) ;
```

7. Save the program as **Lists.java** then compile and run the program to see the output

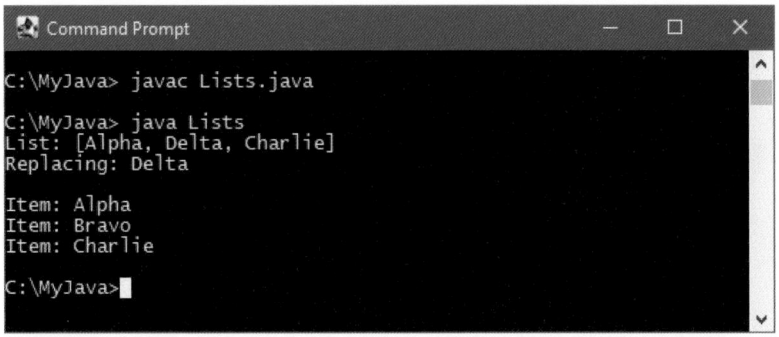

Lists.java

As with regular arrays, elements in an **ArrayList** have a zero-based index.

The graphical Java Swing **JComboBox** component that is introduced on page 143 holds a drop-down list of options, so must also specify its generic data type when that object gets created.

Managing dates

The **java.time** package contains a class named **LocalDateTime** that has useful methods to extract specific fields from a **LocalDateTime** object that describe a particular point in time. These can be made available to a program by importing the specific class with **import java.time.LocalDateTime;** or by importing all classes in this package using the wildcard with **import java.time.* ;** .

A new **LocalDateTime** object can be created with fields describing the current date and time using its **now()** method. The fields are initialized from the system clock for the current locale.

The value within an individual field can be retrieved using an appropriate method of the **LocalDateTime** object. For example, the value of the year field can be retrieved using its **getYear()** method. Similarly, any field can be changed using an appropriate method of the **LocalDateTime** object to specify a replacement value. For example, the value of the year field can be changed by specifying a new year value as an argument to its **withYear()** method.

DateTime.java

1. Start a new program that imports the functionality of all methods in the **java.time.LocalDateTime** class
```
import java.time.LocalDateTime ;
```

2. Add a class named "DateTime" containing the standard main method
```
class DateTime
{
        public static void main ( String [] args ) {        }
}
```

3. Between the curly brackets of the main method, insert a statement to create a current **LocalDateTime** object
```
LocalDateTime date = LocalDateTime.now() ;
```

4. Output the current date and time details
```
System.out.println( "\nIt is now " + date ) ;
```

5. Increment the year, and output the revised date and time
```
date = date.withYear( 2022 ) ;
System.out.println( "\nDate is now " + date ) ;
```

6 Output individual **LocalDateTime** fields of the revised date

```
String fields = "\nYear:\t\t\t" + date.getYear() ;

fields += "\nMonth:\t\t\t" + date.getMonth() ;

fields += "\nMonth Number:\t\t" + date.getMonthValue() ;

fields += "\nDay:\t\t\t" + date.getDayOfWeek() ;

fields += "\nDay Number:\t\t" + date.getDayOfMonth() ;

fields += "\nDay Number Of Year:\t" + date.getDayOfYear() ;

fields += "\nHour (0-23):\t\t" + date.getHour() ;

fields += "\nMinute:\t\t\t" + date.getMinute() ;

fields += "\nSecond:\t\t\t"  + date.getSecond() ;

System.out.println( fields ) ;
```

Concatenating a **String** like this means the program makes just one call to **println()** to output field details – this is more efficient than calling **println()** many times to output each individual field separately.

7 Save the program as **DateTime.java** then compile and run the program to see the output

```
Command Prompt

C:\MyJava> javac DateTime.java

C:\MyJava> java DateTime

It is now 2021-05-20T11:40:26.810717100

Date is now 2022-05-20T11:40:26.810717100

Year:                   2022
Month:                  MAY
Month Number:           5
Day:                    FRIDAY
Day Number:             20
Day Number Of Year:     140
Hour(0-23):             11
Minute:                 40
Second:                 26

C:\MyJava>
```

You can alternatively use the **ZonedDateTime** class instead of **LocalDateTime** if you also require a time zone field.

Formatting numbers

Java contains a package named **java.text** that provides useful classes for formatting numbers and currency. The package can be made available to a program by including an **import** statement at the very beginning of the **.java** file. This can use the * wildcard character to mean "all classes" in the statement **import java.text.* ;**. Alternatively, specific classes can be imported by name.

The **java.text** package has a class named "NumberFormat", which has methods that can be used to format numerical values for output – adding group separators, currency signs, and percentage signs.

The **java.time.format** package was introduced in Java 8 to make it easier to specify date format patterns.

The method used to create a new **NumberFormat** object determines its formatting type – **getNumberInstance()** for group separators, **getCurrencyInstance()** for currency signs, and **getPercentInstance()** for percentage signs. Formatting is applied by specifying the numerical value to be formatted as the argument to the **format()** method of the **NumberFormat** object.

The **java.time.format** package has a **DateTimeFormatter** class that can be used to format **java.time** dates and time objects. A **DateTimeFormatter** object contains a formatter pattern that is specified as a string argument to its **ofPattern()** method. The formatter comprises letters, defined in the Java documentation, and your choice of separators. For example, **"M/d/y"** specifies the month, day, and year, separated by slashes. The format is applied by specifying the formatter as the argument to the **format()** method of a **java.time** date and time object.

Formats.java

1. Start a new program that imports the functionality of all methods of the **NumberFormat** class in the **java.text** package and all methods of the **DateTimeFormatter** class in the **java.time.format** package

```
import java.text.NumberFormat ;
import java.time.format.DateTimeFormatter ;
```

2. Add a class named "Formats" containing the standard main method

```
class Formats
{
        public static void main ( String [] args )
        {

        }
}
```

3. Between the curly brackets of the main method, insert statements to output a number with group separators
```
NumberFormat nf = NumberFormat.getNumberInstance() ;
System.out.println( "\nNumber: " + nf.format(123456789) ) ;
```

4. Add statements to output a number with a currency sign
```
NumberFormat cf = NumberFormat.getCurrencyInstance() ;
System.out.println( "\nCurrency: " + cf.format(1234.50f) ) ;
```

5. Add statements to output a number with a percent sign
```
NumberFormat pf = NumberFormat.getPercentInstance() ;
System.out.println( "\nPercent: " + pf.format( 0.75f ) ) ;
```

6. Add a statement creating a current **LocalDateTime** object
```
java.time.LocalDateTime now =
        java.time.LocalDateTime.now() ;
```

7. Add statements to output a formatted numerical date
```
DateTimeFormatter df =
        DateTimeFormatter.ofPattern( "MMM d, yyy" ) ;
System.out.println( "\nDate: " + now.format( df ) ) ;
```

8. Add statements to output a formatted numerical time
```
DateTimeFormatter tf =
        DateTimeFormatter.ofPattern( "h:m a" ) ;
System.out.println( "\nTime: " + now.format( tf ) ) ;
```

9. Save the program as **Formats.java** then compile and run the program to see the formatted output

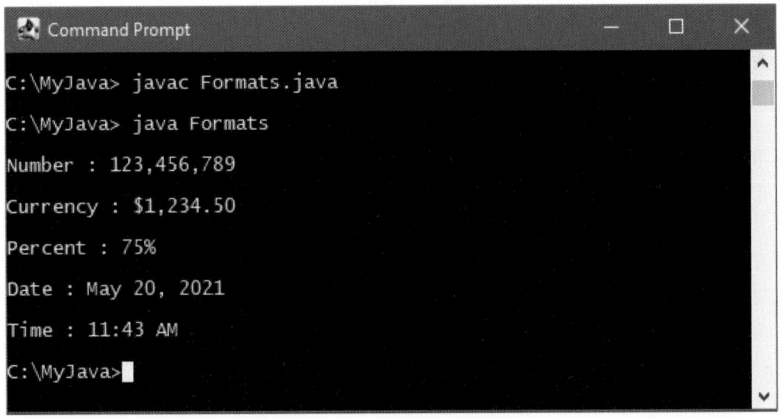

A statement can address a class that has not been imported by using its full package address – as seen here in the statement creating a **LocalDateTime** object.

Pattern letters are case sensitive – refer to the documentation to discover the full details of possible patterns.

Summary

- One or more **import** statements can be included at the start of a program to make the functionality of other classes available.
- An **import** statement can import all classes in a package with a * wildcard character, or individual classes by name.
- The **java.io** package has classes that are designed to handle input and output procedures.
- A **File** object can be used to access files and directories.
- The **InputStreamReader** object decodes input bytes into characters, and the **BufferedReader** reads its decoded characters.
- A **FileReader** object can be used to decode text file bytes into characters for reading by a **BufferedReader** object.
- A **FileWriter** object and **BufferedWriter** object can create and update text files.
- The **java.util** package contains utilities for handling collections of data, such as array manipulation with its **Arrays** class.
- The **java.util** package also contains an **ArrayList** class that has methods to easily manipulate sequenced list items.
- An **ArrayList** object is a Collection that must specify the generic type of item that list may contain, such as **<String>**.
- A lambda expression is an anonymous method that can be specified where it is to be executed.
- The **java.time** package contains a **LocalDateTime** class that provides fields for date and time components.
- The **java.text** package contains a **NumberFormat** class that can format numbers and currency.
- The **java.time.format** package contains a **DateTimeFormatter** class that can specify patterns to format dates and times.

8 Building interfaces

This chapter demonstrates how to use Java Swing components to create a graphical program interface.

134 Creating a window
136 Adding push buttons
138 Adding labels
140 Adding text fields
142 Adding item selectors
144 Adding radio buttons
146 Arranging components
148 Changing appearance
150 Summary

Creating a window

Programs can provide a graphical user interface (GUI) using the "Swing" components of the Java library. The **javax.swing** package contains classes to create a variety of components using the style of the native operating system. These can be made available to a program by including the initial statement **import javax.swing.*;** .

A class must be created to represent the GUI to which components can be added to build the interface. This is easily achieved by declaring it a subclass of Swing's **JFrame** class using the **extends** keyword – thereby inheriting attributes and behaviors that allow the user to move, resize, and close the window.

The class constructor should include statements to set these minimum requirements:

- The title of the window – specified as a **String** argument to the inherited **super()** method of the **JFrame** class.
- The size of the window – specified as width and height in pixels as arguments to its **setSize()** method.
- What to do when the user closes the window – specified as a constant argument to its **setDefaultCloseOperation()** method.
- Display the window – specified as a Boolean argument to its **setVisible()** method.

Remember the letter **x** in **javax.swing** by thinking of **JAVA** e**X**tra.

Additionally, the constructor can add a **JPanel** container component to the window, in which smaller components can be added, using the inherited **add()** method of the **JFrame** class.

By default, a **JPanel** container employs a **FlowLayout** layout manager that lays out components in left-to-right lines, wrapping at the right edge of the window.

Layout managers are described in more detail on page 148.

The steps opposite describe how to create a basic window containing a **JPanel** container with a **FlowLayout** layout manager. This window is featured in subsequent examples in this book that demonstrate how to add various components to the **JPanel** container.

1. Start a new program that imports all Swing components
```
import javax.swing.* ;
```

2. Create a subclass of the **JFrame** class named "Window" containing the standard main method
```
class Window extends JFrame
{
        public static void main ( String[] args ) {          }
}
```

3. Before the main method, create a **JPanel** container object
```
JPanel pnl = new JPanel( ) ;
```

4. Next, insert this constructor method to specify window requirements and to add the **JPanel** object to the **JFrame**
```
public Window()
{
        super( "Swing Window" ) ;
        setSize( 500 , 200 ) ;
        setDefaultCloseOperation( EXIT_ON_CLOSE ) ;
        add( pnl ) ;
        setVisible( true ) ;
}
```

5. Create an instance of the Window class by inserting this line into the main method
```
Window gui = new Window() ;
```

6. Save the program as **Window.java** then compile and run the program to see the basic window appear

Window.java

The **EXIT_ON_CLOSE** operation is a constant member of the **JFrame** class. It exits the program when the window gets closed.

Notice how the **add()** method is used here to add the **JPanel** object to the **JFrame** window.

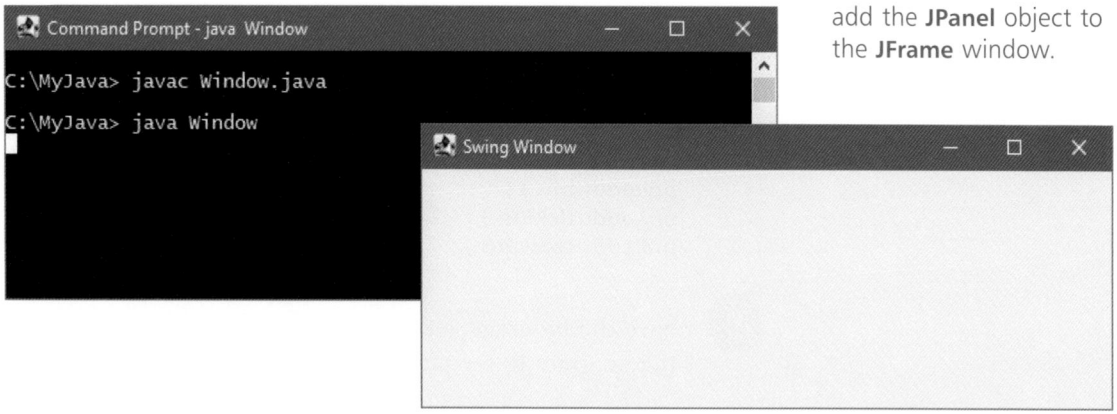

Adding push buttons

The Swing **JButton** class creates a push-button component that can be added to a graphical interface. This lets the user interact with the program by clicking on a button to perform an action.

The **JButton** object is created with the **new** keyword, and its constructor takes a **String** argument specifying text to be displayed on that button.

Images can appear on buttons too. An **ImageIcon** object must first be created to represent the image, specifying the image file name as the argument to its constructor. Typically, the image will be located alongside the program but the argument can include the path for images outside the local directory.

Specify the name of the **ImageIcon** object as the argument to the **JButton** constructor to display that image on the button, or specify a **String** and **ImageIcon** as its two arguments to display both text and the image.

The next chapter, Chapter 9, details of how to create event-handler methods to respond to user actions, such as a button click.

Buttons.java

1. Edit a copy of **Window.java** from page 135, changing the class name in the declaration, the constructor, and the instance statement from "Window" to "Buttons"

2. Before the **Buttons()** constructor, create two **ImageIcon** objects
```
ImageIcon tick = new ImageIcon( "Tick.png" ) ;
ImageIcon cross = new ImageIcon( "Cross.png" ) ;
```

3. Next, create three **JButton** objects to display text, an image, and both text and an image respectively
```
JButton btn = new JButton( "Click Me" ) ;
JButton tickBtn = new JButton( tick ) ;
JButton crossBtn = new JButton( "STOP" , cross ) ;
```

4. Inside the **Buttons()** constructor, insert three statements to add the **JButton** components to the **JPanel** container
```
pnl.add( btn ) ;
pnl.add( tickBtn ) ;
pnl.add( crossBtn ) ;
```

5. Save the program as **Buttons.java** then compile and run the program to see push buttons appear in the window

The **JPanel** object has an **add()** method – to add components to that panel.

Details of how to create a Java Archive (JAR) can be found on page 172.

The buttons respond graphically when they are clicked, but will not perform an action until the program provides an event-handler method to respond to each click event.

Where the program is intended for deployment in a single Java archive (JAR), image resources must be loaded by a **ClassLoader** object before creating the **ImageIcon** objects to represent them.

Specifying the resource file name or path to the **getResource()** method of a **ClassLoader** returns a URL, which can be used as the argument to the **ImageIcon** constructor. The **java.net** package provides a useful **URL** class to which these may first be assigned.

6. Before the **Buttons()** constructor, create a **ClassLoader** object
```
ClassLoader ldr = this.getClass().getClassLoader() ;
```

7. Load the URLs of the image resources
```
java.net.URL tickURL = ldr.getResource( "Tick.png" ) ;
java.net.URL crossURL = ldr.getResource( "Cross.png" ) ;
```

8. Edit the **ImageIcon()** constructors in Step 2 opposite to use URLs
```
ImageIcon tick = new ImageIcon( tickURL ) ;
ImageIcon cross = new ImageIcon( crossURL ) ;
```

9. Save the changes then recompile and re-run the program – it will run as before but can now be deployed in a JAR

Notice how the **getClass()** method and **this** keyword are used here to reference this class object.

Adding labels

The Swing **JLabel** class creates a label component that can be added to a graphical interface. This can be used to display non-interactive text or image, or both text and an image.

The **JLabel** object is created with the **new** keyword, and its constructor takes a **String** argument specifying text to be displayed on that label, or the name of an **ImageIcon** object representing an image to display. It can also take three arguments to specify text, image, and horizontal alignment as a **JLabel** constant value. For example, **JLabel("text", img, JLabel.CENTER)** aligns centrally.

Where a **JLabel** object contains both text and an image, the relative position of the text can be determined by specifying a **JLabel** constant as the argument to **setVerticalPosition()** and **setHorizontalPosition()** methods of the **JLabel** object.

Additionally, a **JLabel** object can be made to display a ToolTip when the cursor hovers over, by specifying a text **String** as the argument to that object's **setToolTipText()** method.

Labels.java

1. Edit a copy of **Window.java** from page 135, changing the class name in the declaration, the constructor, and the instance statement from "Window" to "Labels"

2. Before the **Labels()** constructor, create an **ImageIcon** object
```
ImageIcon duke = new ImageIcon( "Duke.png" ) ;
```

3. Next, create three **JLabel** objects to display an image, text, and both text and an image respectively
```
JLabel lbl1 = new JLabel( duke ) ;
JLabel lbl2 = new JLabel( "Duke is the friendly mascot
                                    of Java technology." ) ;
JLabel lbl3 = new JLabel( "Duke" , duke , JLabel.CENTER ) ;
```

4. Inside the **Labels()** constructor, insert this statement to create a ToolTip for the first label
```
lbl1.setToolTipText( "Duke - the Java Mascot" ) ;
```

5. Add these two statements to align the text centrally below the third label
```
lbl3.setHorizontalTextPosition( JLabel.CENTER ) ;
lbl3.setVerticalTextPosition( JLabel.BOTTOM ) ;
```

6. Now, add three statements to add the **JLabel** components to the **JPanel** container

```
pnl.add( lbl1 ) ;
pnl.add( lbl2 ) ;
pnl.add( lbl3 ) ;
```

7. Save the program as **Labels.java** then compile and run the program, placing the cursor over the first label

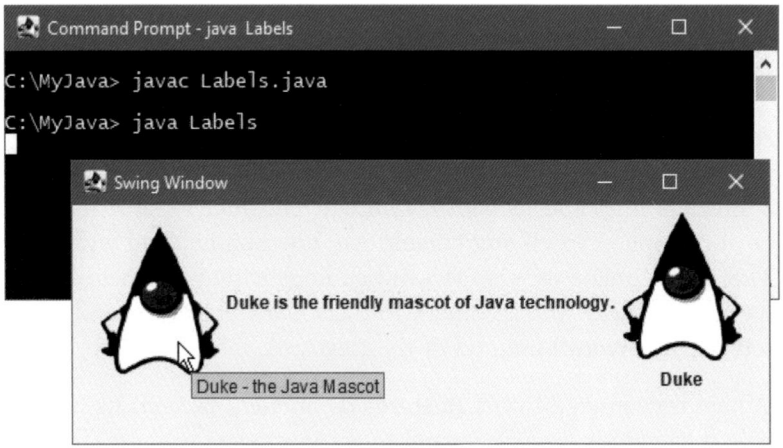

JLabel alignment constants include **LEFT**, **CENTER**, **RIGHT**, **TOP** and **BOTTOM**.

Where the program is intended for deployment in a single Java archive (JAR), the image resource must be loaded by a **ClassLoader** object before creating the **ImageIcon** object to represent it.

Specifying the resource file name or path to the **getResource()** method of a **ClassLoader** returns a URL, which can be used as the argument to the **ImageIcon** constructor.

8. Before the **Labels()** constructor, create a **ClassLoader** object

```
ClassLoader ldr = this.getClass().getClassLoader() ;
```

9. Edit the **ImageIcon()** constructor in Step 2 opposite to load the URL of the image resource using the **ClassLoader** object

```
ImageIcon duke =
        new ImageIcon( ldr.getResource( "Duke.png" ) ) ;
```

10. Save the changes, then recompile and re-run the program – it will run as before, but can now be deployed in a JAR

Details of how to create a Java Archive (JAR) can be found on page 172.

Adding text fields

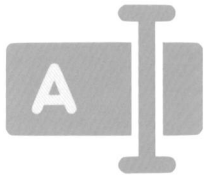

The Swing **JTextField** class creates a single-line text field component that can be added to a graphical interface. This can be used to display editable text, and allows the user to enter text to interact with the program.

The **JTextField** object is created with the **new** keyword, and its constructor can take a **String** argument specifying default text to be displayed in that field. In this case, the component will be sized to accommodate the length of the **String**. Alternatively, the argument may be a numeric value to specify the text field size. The constructor can also take two arguments, specifying both default text and the text field size.

A multiple-line text field can be created with the **JTextArea** class, whose constructor takes two numerical arguments specifying its number of lines and its width. Alternatively, three arguments can be supplied specifying default text, line number, and width. Text can be made to wrap at word endings within this field by specifying **true** as the argument to the **setLineWrap()** method and **setWrapStyleWord()** method of the **JTextArea** object.

Use the **JPasswordField** class instead of the **JTextField** class where input characters are needed to be not visible.

Where text entered into a **JTextArea** component exceeds its initial size, the component will expand to accommodate the text. To make the component a fixed size with scrolling capability, it can be placed in a **JScrollPane** container. This is created with the **new** keyword, and takes the name of the **JTextArea** as its argument.

Scroll bars will, by default, only appear when the field contains text that exceeds its initial size – but they can be made to appear constantly by specifying a **JScrollPane** constant as the argument to the snappily-named **setVerticalScrollBarPolicy()** or **setHorizontalScrollBarPolicy()** methods of the **JScrollPane** object. For example, to always display a vertical scrollbar use the **JScrollPane.VERTICAL_SCROLLBAR_ALWAYS** constant as the argument.

TextFields.java

1. Edit a copy of **Window.java** from page 135, changing the class name in the declaration, the constructor, and the instance statement from "Window" to "TextFields"

2. Before the **TextFields()** constructor, create two **JTextField** objects

```
JTextField txt1 = new JTextField( 38 ) ;
JTextField txt2 = new JTextField( "Default Text" , 38 ) ;
```

3. Create a **JTextArea** object five lines high
```
JTextArea txtArea = new JTextArea( 5 , 37 ) ;
```

4. Add a **JScrollPane** object – to contain the **JTextArea** created in Step 3, above
```
JScrollPane pane = new JScrollPane( txtArea ) ;
```

5. In the **TextFields()** constructor method, insert statements to enable the **JTextArea** object to wrap at word endings
```
txtArea.setLineWrap( true ) ;
txtArea.setWrapStyleWord( true ) ;
```

6. Insert a statement to always display a vertical scrollbar for the **JTextArea** object
```
pane.setVerticalScrollBarPolicy
        ( JScrollPane.VERTICAL_SCROLLBAR_ALWAYS ) ;
```

7. Insert two statements to add the **JTextField** components to the **JPanel** container
```
pnl.add( txt1 ) ;
pnl.add( txt2 ) ;
```

8. Insert another statement to add the **JScrollPane** container, (containing the **JTextArea** field) to the **JPanel** container
```
pnl.add( pane ) ;
```

9. Save the program as **TextFields.java** then compile and run the program, entering some text into the text area

A **JTextArea** component has no scrolling ability unless it is contained within a **JScrollPane** component.

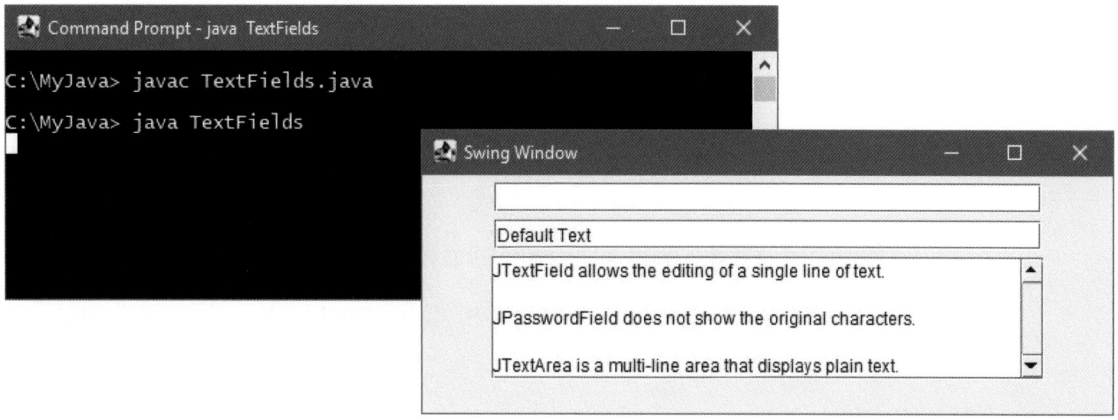

Adding item selectors

The Swing **JCheckBox** class creates a checkbox component that can be added to a graphical interface. This can be used to allow the user to select or deselect individual items in a program. The **JCheckBox** object is created with the **new** keyword, and its constructor takes a **String** argument specifying text to be displayed alongside that checkbox. It can also take a second **true** argument to make the checkbox be selected by default.

A choice of items can be offered by the **JComboBox** class that creates a drop-down list from which the user can select any single item. This object is created with the **new** keyword, and its constructor typically takes the name of a **String** array as its argument. Each element in the array provides an item for selection in the drop-down list. Similarly, a choice of items can be offered by the **JList** class that creates a fixed-size list from which the user can select one or more items. It is created with the **new** keyword, and its constructor also takes an array as its argument, with each element providing an item for selection. As both **JList** and **JComboBox** are "Collections" they must specify the generic type they may contain when they get created, such as **<String>**.

Items.java

1. Edit a copy of **Window.java** from page 135, changing the class name in the declaration, the constructor, and the instance statement from "Window" to "Items"

2. Before the **Items()** constructor, create a **String** array of items for selection

```
String[] toppings =
        { "Pepperoni" , "Mushroom" , "Ham" , "Tomato" } ;
```

3. Next, create four **JCheckBox** objects to present each array item for selection – with one selected by default

```
JCheckBox chk1 = new JCheckBox( toppings[0] ) ;
JCheckBox chk2 = new JCheckBox( toppings[1] , true ) ;
JCheckBox chk3 = new JCheckBox( toppings[2] ) ;
JCheckBox chk4 = new JCheckBox( toppings[3] ) ;
```

4. Add a second **String** array of items for selection

```
String[] styles =
        { "Deep Dish" , "Gourmet Style" , "Thin & Crispy" } ;
```

5. Create a **JComboBox** object to present each item in the second array for selection

```
JComboBox<String> box1 =
        new JComboBox<String>( styles ) ;
```

6. Add a **JList** object to present each item in the first array for selection from a list

```
JList<String> lst1 = new JList<String>( toppings ) ;
```

7. In the **Items()** constructor method, insert statements to add each **JCheckBox** component to the **JPanel** container

```
pnl.add( chk1 ) ;
pnl.add( chk2 ) ;
pnl.add( chk3 ) ;
pnl.add( chk4 ) ;
```

8. Insert statements to make a default selection and to add the **JComboBox** component to the **JPanel** container

```
box1.setSelectedIndex( 0 ) ;
pnl.add( box1 ) ;
```

9. Now, insert a statement to add the **JList** component to the **JPanel** container

```
pnl.add( lst1 ) ;
```

10. Save the program as **Items.java** then compile and run the program, selecting items from the lists

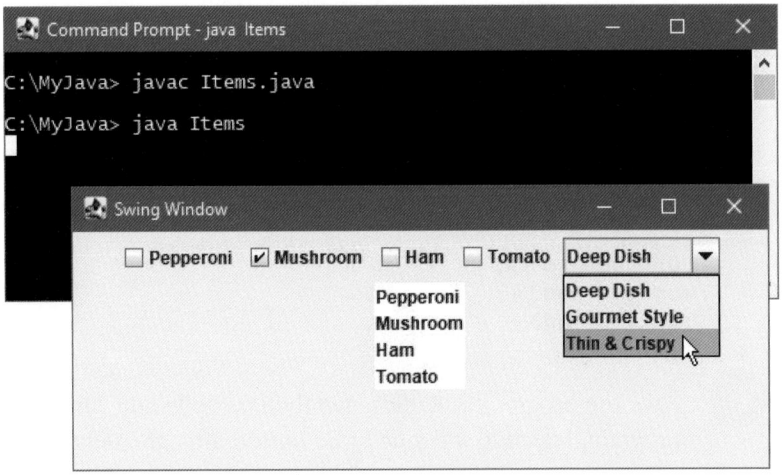

Only one item can be selected from a **JComboBox** component – multiple items can be selected from a **JList** component.

Details of how to create event-handler methods to respond to user actions, such as an item selection, can be found in Chapter 9.

Adding radio buttons

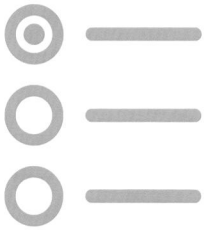

The Swing **JRadioButton** class creates a radio button component that can be added to a graphical interface. This can be used to allow the user to select an item from a group of radio buttons.

The **JRadioButton** object is created with the **new** keyword, and its constructor takes a **String** argument specifying text to be displayed alongside that radio button. It can also take a second **true** argument to make a radio button be selected by default.

A **ButtonGroup** object logically groups a number of radio buttons so that only one button in that group can be selected at any time. Each radio button is added to the **ButtonGroup** object by specifying its name as the argument to the group's **add()** method.

Radios.java

1. Edit a copy of **Window.java** from page 135, changing the class name in the declaration, the constructor, and the instance statement from "Window" to "Radios"

2. Before the **Radios()** constructor, create three **JRadioButton** objects – with one selected by default
```
JRadioButton rad1 = new JRadioButton( "Red" , true  ) ;
JRadioButton rad2 = new JRadioButton( "Rosé" ) ;
JRadioButton rad3 = new JRadioButton( "White" ) ;
```

3. Next, create a **ButtonGroup** object with which to group the radio buttons
```
ButtonGroup wines = new ButtonGroup() ;
```

The **ButtonGroup** object only groups the buttons logically, not physically.

4. In the **Radios()** constructor method, insert statements to add each **JRadioButton** component to the **JButtonGroup**
```
wines.add( rad1 ) ;
wines.add( rad2 ) ;
wines.add( rad3 ) ;
```

5. Insert statements to add the **JRadioButton** components to the **JPanel** container
```
pnl.add( rad1 ) ;
pnl.add( rad2 ) ;
pnl.add( rad3 ) ;
```

6. Save the program as **Radios.java** then compile and run the program, selecting any one radio button after the default

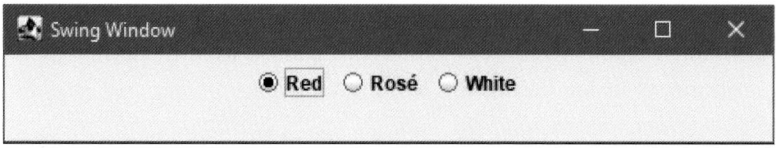

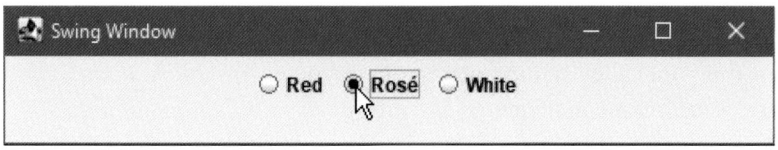

The examples on the previous pages have demonstrated the most common Swing components – **JButton**, **JLabel**, **JTextField**, **JCheckBox**, **JComboBox**, **JList** and **JRadioButton**. There are many more specialized components available in the **javax.swing** package, whose details can be found in the Java documentation – for example, the **JSlider**, **JProgressBar**, and **JMenuBar** components below:

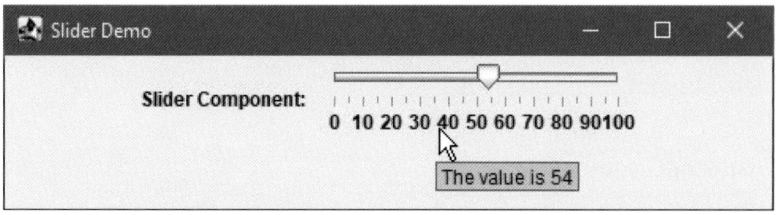

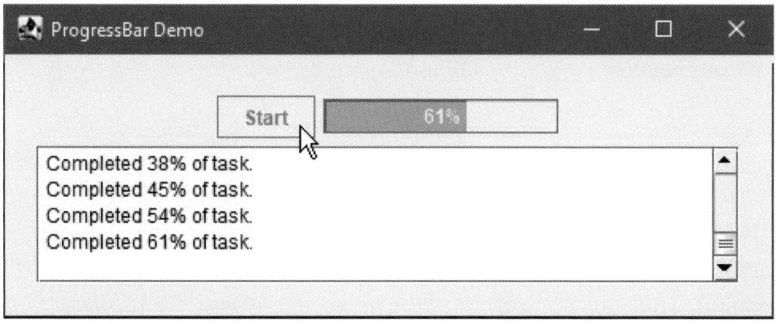

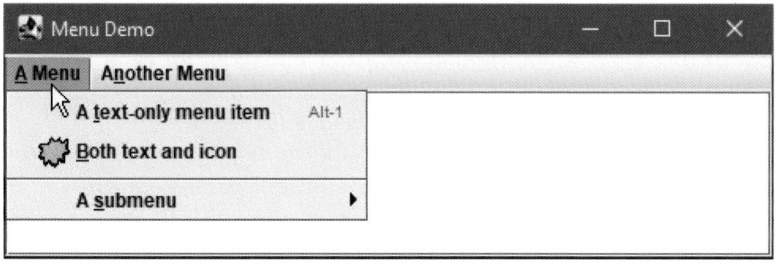

Details of how to create event-handler methods to respond to user actions can be found in Chapter 9.

Try using the Java documentation to add a **JSlider** component to the Radios program – see page 80 for details on how to use the documentation.

Arranging components

The **java.awt** package (Abstract Window Toolkit) contains a number of layout manager classes that can be used to place components in a container in different ways.

A layout manager object is created using the **new** keyword, and can then be specified as the argument to a **JPanel** constructor to have the panel use that layout. When components get added to the panel they will be placed according to the rules of the specified layout manager.

Layout Manager:	Rules:
BorderLayout	Places North, South, East, West and Center (the content pane default)
BoxLayout	Places in a single row or column
CardLayout	Places different components in a specified area at different times
FlowLayout	Places left to right in a wrapping line (the **JPanel** default)
GridBagLayout	Places in a grid of cells, allowing components to span cells
GridLayout	Places in a grid of rows and columns
GroupLayout	Places horizontally and vertically
SpringLayout	Places by relative spacing

You can find further details of each layout manager in the **java.awt** section of the Java documentation.

The top level **JFrame** object has a "content pane" container that places components using the **BorderLayout** layout manager by default. This can be used to place up to five **JPanel** containers, which may each use their default **FlowLayout** layout manager or any of the layout managers in the table above. Using a variety of layout managers accommodates most layout requirements.

The content pane can be represented by a **java.awt.Container** object, whose **add()** method can specify the position and name of a component to be placed within the content pane.

1. Edit a copy of **Window.java** from page 135, changing the class declaration, constructor, and instance from "Window" to "Layout", then add a statement at the start of the program to import the functionality of the **java.awt** package
```
import java.awt.* ;
```

Layout.java

2. Before the **Layout()** constructor, create a **Container** object representing the **JFrame** content pane container
```
Container contentPane = getContentPane() ;
```

3. Create a second **JPanel** object using a **GridLayout** layout manager in a 2 x 2 grid
```
JPanel grid = new JPanel( new GridLayout( 2 , 2 ) ) ;
```

4. In the **Layout()** constructor method, insert statements adding **JButton** components to both **JPanel** objects
```
pnl.add( new JButton( "Yes" ) ) ;
pnl.add( new JButton( "No" ) ) ;
pnl.add( new JButton( "Cancel" ) ) ;
grid.add( new JButton( "1" ) ) ;
grid.add( new JButton( "2" ) ) ;
grid.add( new JButton( "3" ) ) ;
grid.add( new JButton( "4" ) ) ;
```

5. Now, insert statements adding both panels and a button to the content pane
```
contentPane.add( "North" , pnl ) ;
contentPane.add( "Center" , grid ) ;
contentPane.add( "West" , new JButton( "West" ) ) ;
```

6. Save the program as **Layout.java** then compile and run the program to see the component layout

While the **FlowLayout** maintains the **JButton** size, other layout managers expand the components to fill their layout design.

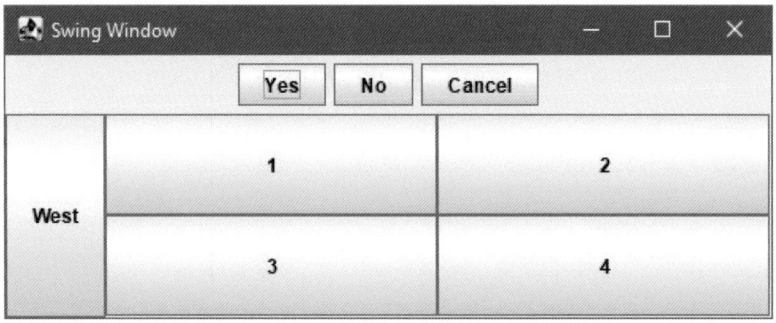

Changing appearance

The **java.awt** package (Abstract Window Toolkit) contains "painting" classes that can be used to color interface components. These can be made available to a program by including the initial statement **import java.awt.* ;** .

Included in the **java.awt** package is a **Color** class that has constants representing a few basic colors, such as **Color.RED**. Additionally, instances of the **Color** class can be created using the **new** keyword to represent custom colors. The constructor can take three integer arguments between zero and 255 to represent red, green, and blue (RGB) values to form the custom color.

Each component has a **setBackground()** method and a **setForeground()** method that take a **Color** object as their argument to paint that component with the specified color.

Note that the background of **JLabel** components are transparent by default, so it is recommended that their **setOpaque()** method should be called to set the opacity to **true** before they are painted.

Also in the **java.awt** package is a **Font** class that can be used to modify the font displaying text. A **Font** object represents a font, and its constructor can take three arguments to specify name, style and size:

- The specified name should be one of the three platform-independent names "Serif", "SansSerif" or "Monospaced".
- The specified style should be one of the following three constants: **Font.PLAIN**, **Font.BOLD** or **Font.ITALIC**.
- The specified size should be an integer of the point size.

Each component has a **setFont()** method that takes a **Font** object as its argument to paint that component with the specified font.

Custom.java

1. Edit a copy of **Window.java** from page 135, changing the class name in the declaration, the constructor, and the instance statement from "Window" to "Custom"

2. Add a statement at the very start of the program to import the functionality of all classes in the **java.awt** package
import java.awt.* ;

3. Before the **Custom()** constructor, create three **JLabel** objects
```
JLabel lbl1 = new JLabel( "Custom Background" ) ;
JLabel lbl2 = new JLabel( "Custom Foreground" ) ;
JLabel lbl3 = new JLabel( "Custom Font" ) ;
```

4. Next, create **Color**, **Font**, and **Box** layout objects
```
Color customColor = new Color( 255 , 0 , 0 ) ;
Font customFont = new Font( "Serif" , Font.PLAIN , 64 ) ;
Box box = Box.createVerticalBox() ;
```

5. In the **Custom()** constructor method, insert statements to color a **JLabel** background using a **Color** constant
```
lbl1.setOpaque( true ) ;
lbl1.setBackground( Color.YELLOW ) ;
```

6. Insert a statement to color a **JLabel** foreground using a custom **Color** object
```
lbl2.setForeground( customColor ) ;
```

7. Insert a statement to paint text on a **JLabel** component using a custom font
```
lbl3.setFont( customFont ) ;
```

8. Add each label to the layout container
```
box.add( lbl1 ) ; box.add( lbl2 ) ; box.add( lbl3 ) ;
```

9. Then, add the layout container to the **JPanel** container
```
pnl.add( box ) ;
```

10. Save the program as **Custom.java** then compile and run the program to see the effect

In this case, the custom color is equivalent to **Color.RED**, as the RGB value specifies the maximum red value with no green or blue.

A **Box** object is a handy lightweight container that uses **BoxLayout** as its layout manager. The **Box** object's **createVerticalBox()** method individually displays its components from top to bottom.

Summary

- The **javax.swing** package contains the Java Swing classes that are used to create GUI components.
- A window is created as a top-level **JFrame** container.
- The **JFrame** constructor should specify the window's title, size, default close operation and visibility.
- A **JPanel** container displays smaller components in a wrapping line using its default **FlowLayout** layout manager.
- The **JButton** constructor can specify text and images to be displayed on a push-button component.
- An **ImageIcon** object represents an image to use in the program.
- Programs that are to be deployed as a single Java archive (JAR) should use a **ClassLoader** object to specify an image source.
- A **JLabel** object displays non-interactive text and image content.
- Editable text can be displayed in **JTextField** and **JTextArea** fields.
- A **JScrollPane** object provides scrollbars for a **JTextArea** field.
- Items for selection can be displayed with **JCheckBox**, **JComboBox** and **JList** components.
- A **ButtonGroup** object logically groups a number of **JRadioButton** components so only one can be selected.
- Specific RGB colors can be represented by the **Color** class of the **java.awt** package.
- The **java.awt** package has a **Font** class that can be used to create objects representing a particular font name, style, and size.
- Multiple **JPanel** containers can be added to a **JFrame** container by using the **Container** class of the **java.awt** package to represent the content pane of the **JFrame**.
- When creating a **JPanel** container object, its argument may optionally specify a layout manager.

9 Recognizing events

This chapter demonstrates how to create Java program event-handlers that respond to user interface actions.

152 Listening for events

153 Generating events

154 Handling button events

156 Handling item events

158 Reacting to keyboard events

160 Responding to mouse events

162 Announcing messages

164 Requesting input

166 Summary

Listening for events

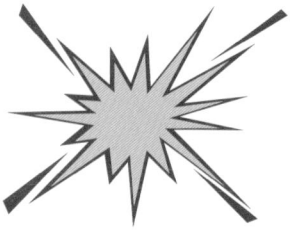

A user can interact with a program that provides a graphical user interface (GUI) by performing actions with a mouse, keyboard, or other input device. These actions cause "events" to occur in the interface, and making a program respond to them is known as "event-handling".

For a program to recognize user events it needs to have one or more **EventListener** interfaces added from the **java.awt.event** package. These can be made available to the program by adding an initial statement to **import java.awt.event.* ;** .

The desired **EventListener** interface can be included in the class declaration using the **implements** keyword. For example, a class declaration to listen for button clicks might look like this:

```
class Click extends JFrame implements ActionListener {   }
```

The Java documentation describes many **EventListener** interfaces that can listen out for different events, but the most common ones are listed in the table below, together with a brief description:

EventListener:	Description:
ActionListener	Recognizes action events that occur when a push button is pushed or released
ItemListener	Recognizes item events that occur when a list item gets selected or deselected
KeyListener	Recognizes keyboard events that occur when the user presses or releases a key
MouseListener	Recognizes mouse button actions that occur when the user presses or releases a mouse button, and when the mouse enters or exits a component
MouseMotionListener	Recognizes motion events that occur when the user moves the mouse

Multiple EventListeners can be included after the **implements** keyword as a comma-separated list.

Generating events

Components need to generate events that the **EventListener** interfaces can recognize if they are to be useful. Having added the appropriate **EventListener** to the program, as described opposite, an event generator must be added to the component.

For example, in order to have the program respond to a button click, the **ActionListener** interface is added to the program and the button's **addActionListener()** method must be called, specifying the **this** keyword as its argument. This makes the button generate an event when it gets clicked, which can be recognized by the **ActionListener** interface.

Statements creating a button that generates events look like this:

```
JButton btn = new JButton( "Click Me" ) ;
btn.addActionListener( this ) ;
```

When the user clicks a button that generates an event, the **ActionListener** interface recognizes the event and seeks an event-handler method within the program to execute a response.

Each **EventListener** interface has an associated event-handler method that is called when an event is recognized. For example, when a button gets clicked, the **ActionListener** interface calls an associated method named **actionPerformed()** and passes an **ActionEvent** object as its argument.

An **ActionEvent** object contains information about the event and the source component from where it originated. Most usefully, it has a **getSource()** method that identifies the object that generated the event. This can be used to create an appropriate response for that component.

An event-handler method to create a response for a specific button click could look like this:

```
public void actionPerformed( ActionEvent event )
{
        if ( event.getSource() == btn )
        {
                Statements to be executed for this button click event
        }
}
```

Handling button events

A Swing **JButton** component that is set to generate an **ActionEvent** event when it gets clicked can be recognized by the **ActionListener** interface, which will pass the event to its **actionPerformed()** event-handler method. The **ActionEvent** object has a **getSource()** method that identifies the originating component, and a **getActionCommand()** method that returns a **String**. This will be the text label for a button component, or the content for a text field component.

One response to a button might be to disable a component by calling its **setEnabled()** method with a **false** argument. Conversely, the component can be enabled once more by specifying a **true** argument to its **setEnabled()** method.

Actions.java

1. Edit a copy of **Window.java** from page 135, changing the class name in the declaration, the constructor, and the instance statement from "Window" to "Actions"

2. Add a statement at the very start of the program to import the functionality of all classes in the **java.awt.event** package
```
import java.awt.event.* ;
```

3. Edit the class declaration to add an **ActionListener** interface to the program
```
class Actions extends JFrame implements ActionListener
```

4. Before the **Actions()** constructor, create two **JButton** push buttons and a **JTextArea** text field
```
JButton btn1 = new JButton( "Button 1" ) ;
JButton btn2 = new JButton( "Button 2" ) ;
JTextArea txtArea = new JTextArea( 5 , 38 ) ;
```

5. Add the buttons and text area to the **JPanel** container
```
pnl.add( btn1 ) ;
pnl.add( btn2 ) ;
pnl.add( txtArea ) ;
```

6. Insert statements to set the initial state of two components
```
btn2.setEnabled( false ) ;
txtArea.setText( "Button 2 is Disabled" ) ;
```

7. In the **Actions()** constructor, insert statements to make each button generate an **ActionEvent event** when clicked

```
btn1.addActionListener( this ) ;
btn2.addActionListener( this ) ;
```

8. After the constructor method, add an event-handler method for the **ActionListener** interface – to display text identifying which button has been clicked

```
public void actionPerformed( ActionEvent event )
{
        txtArea.setText( event.getActionCommand()
                        + " Clicked and Disabled" ) ;
}
```

9. Insert **if** statements in the event-handler method – executing a specific response to each button click

```
if ( event.getSource() == btn1 )
{ btn2.setEnabled( true ) ; btn1.setEnabled( false ) ;      }

if ( event.getSource() == btn2 )
{ btn1.setEnabled( true ) ; btn2.setEnabled( false ) ;      }
```

10. Save the program as **Actions.java** then compile and run the program, clicking the push buttons

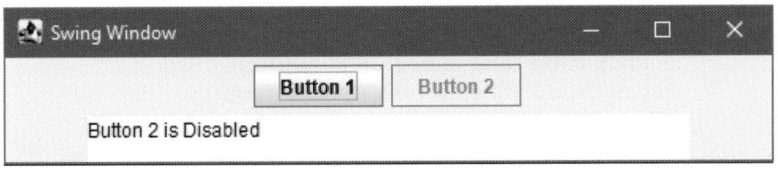

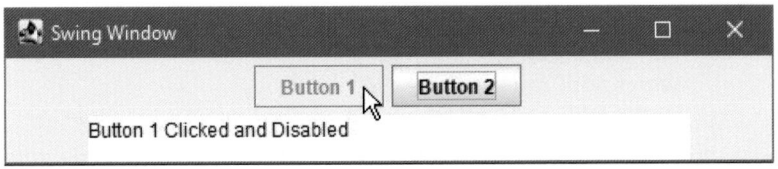

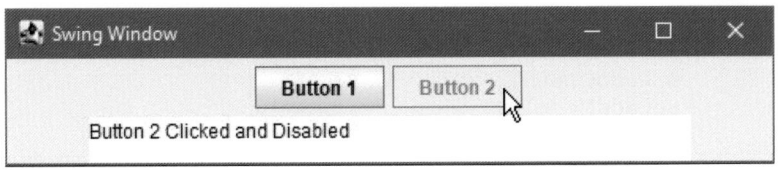

The components are declared before the constructor so they are globally accessible to the event-handler method.

It's sometimes useful to disable a component until the user has performed a required action.

Handling item events

Swing **JRadioButton**, **JCheckBox** and **JComboBox** components maintain states whose change can be recognized by the **ItemListener** interface, which will pass the **ItemEvent** to its **itemStateChanged()** event-handler method. The **ItemEvent** object has a **getItemSelectable()** method that identifies the originating component, and a **getStateChange()** method that returns its status. This will determine if the change is selecting or deselecting an item, and can be compared to an **ItemEvent.SELECTED** constant.

States.java

1. Edit a copy of **Window.java** from page 135, changing the class name in the declaration, the constructor, and the instance statement from "Window" to "States". Then, add a statement at the very start of the program to import the functionality of the **java.awt.event** package

```
import java.awt.event.* ;
```

2. Edit the class declaration to add an **ItemListener** interface to the program

```
class States extends JFrame implements ItemListener
```

3. Before the **States()** constructor, create these components

```
String[] styles =
   { "Deep Dish" , "Gourmet Style" , "Thin & Crispy" } ;
JComboBox<String> box =
   new JComboBox<String> ( styles ) ;
JRadioButton rad1 = new JRadioButton( "White" ) ;
JRadioButton rad2 = new JRadioButton( "Red" ) ;
ButtonGroup wines = new ButtonGroup() ;
JCheckBox chk = new JCheckBox( "Pepperoni" ) ;
JTextArea txtArea = new JTextArea( 5 , 38 ) ;
```

Note how this example uses the **append()** method to add further text to the text area.

4. In the **States()** constructor, insert statements to group the two **JRadioButton** components

```
wines.add( rad1 ) ;
wines.add( rad2 ) ;
```

5. Insert statements to add the components to the **JPanel** container

```
pnl.add( rad1 ) ;
pnl.add( rad2 ) ;
pnl.add( chk ) ;
pnl.add( box ) ;
pnl.add( txtArea ) ;
```

6. Insert statements to make selectable components generate an **ItemEvent** event when an item is selected or deselected

```
rad1.addItemListener( this ) ;
rad2.addItemListener( this ) ;
chk.addItemListener( this ) ;
box.addItemListener( this ) ;
```

7. After the constructor method, add an event-handler method for the **ItemListener** interface – identifying items selected by the **JRadioButton** components

```
public void itemStateChanged( ItemEvent event )
{
        if ( event.getItemSelectable() == rad1 )
        txtArea.setText( "White wine selected" ) ;

        if ( event.getItemSelectable() == rad2 )
        txtArea.setText( "Red wine selected" ) ;
}
```

8. Add an **if** statement to the event-handler method to indicate the status of the **JCheckBox** component

```
if ( ( event.getItemSelectable() == chk ) &&
  ( event.getStateChange() == ItemEvent.SELECTED ) )
txtArea.append( "\nPepperoni selected\n" ) ;
```

9. Add an **if** statement to the event-handler method to indicate the status of the **JComboBox** component

```
if ( ( event.getItemSelectable() == box ) &&
  ( event.getStateChange() == ItemEvent.SELECTED ) )
txtArea.append( event.getItem().toString() + " selected" ) ;
```

10. Save the program as **States.java** then compile and run the program, selecting various items from left to right

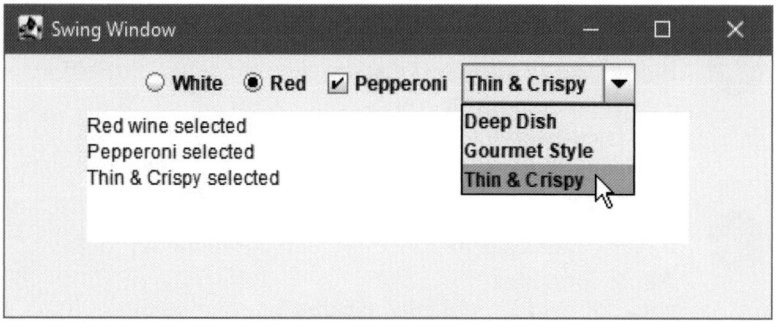

The **JComboBox** fires two ItemEvents when an item gets selected – one selecting the item and one deselecting the previously selected item. That is why Steps 8 and 9 must identify both the originating component and the type of **ItemEvent**.

Notice that the **getItem()** method returns the item affected by the change.

Reacting to keyboard events

Swing components that allow the user to input text can recognize user key strokes with the **KeyListener** interface, which will pass the **KeyEvent** event to these three event-handler methods:

Event-handler:	Description:
keyPressed(KeyEvent)	Called when a key is pressed
keyTyped(KeyEvent)	Called after a key is pressed
keyReleased(KeyEvent)	Called when a key is released

When a program implements the **KeyListener** interface it must declare these three methods – even if not all are actually used.

The **KeyEvent** object has a **getKeyChar()** method, which returns the character for that key, and a **getKeyCode()** method, which returns an integer Unicode value representing that key. Additionally, a **getKeyText()** method takes the key code value as its argument and returns a description of that key.

Keystrokes.java

1. Edit a copy of **Window.java** from page 135, changing the class name in the declaration, the constructor, and the instance statement from "Window" to "Keystrokes". Then, add an initial statement to import the functionality of the **java.awt.event** package
```
import java.awt.event.* ;
```

2. Edit the class declaration to add a **KeyListener** interface to the program
```
class Keystrokes extends JFrame implements KeyListener
```

3. Before the **Keystrokes()** constructor, create a **JTextField** component and a **JTextArea** component
```
JTextField field = new JTextField( 38 ) ;
JTextArea txtArea = new JTextArea( 5 , 38 ) ;
```

4. Insert statements to add these two components to the **JPanel** container
```
pnl.add( field ) ;  pnl.add( txtArea ) ;
```

5. In the **Keystrokes()** constructor, insert a statement to make the **JTextField** component generate **KeyEvent** events

```
field.addKeyListener( this ) ;
```

6. After the constructor method, add an event-handler that acknowledges when a key gets pressed

```
public void keyPressed( KeyEvent event )
{
        txtArea.setText( "Key Pressed" ) ;
}
```

7. Add a second event-handler that displays the key character after the key has been pressed

```
public void keyTyped( KeyEvent event )
{
        txtArea.append( "\nCharacter : "
                                + event.getKeyChar() ) ;
}
```

8. Add a third event-handler that displays the key code and key text when the key gets released

```
public void keyReleased( KeyEvent event )
{
        int keyCode = event.getKeyCode() ;
        txtArea.append( "\nKey Code : "
                                + keyCode ) ;
        txtArea.append( "\nKey Text : "
                        + event.getKeyText( keyCode ) ) ;
}
```

9. Save the program as **Keystrokes.java** then compile and run the program, typing in the top text field

The **getKeyCode()** method only returns the key code if called from within the **keyPressed()** or **keyReleased()** event-handlers – not from the **keyTyped()** event-handler.

Run this program and press a non-character key, such as Backspace, to see its key text name.

Responding to mouse events

Swing components can recognize user mouse actions with the **MouseListener** interface, which will pass the **MouseEvent** event to these five event-handler methods:

Event-handler:	Description:
mousePressed(MouseEvent)	Button is pressed
mouseReleased(MouseEvent)	Button is released
mouseClicked(MouseEvent)	Button has been released
mouseEntered(MouseEvent)	Mouse moves on
mouseExited(MouseEvent)	Mouse moves off

Mouse movements can be recognized by the **MouseMotionListener** interface, which passes **MouseEvent** events to two event-handlers:

Event-handler:	Description:
mouseMoved(MouseEvent)	Mouse is moved
mouseDragged(MouseEvent)	Mouse is dragged

When a program implements the **MouseListener** or **MouseMotionListener** interface, it must declare all its associated event-handler methods – even if not all are actually used.

The **MouseEvent** object passed by the **MouseMotionListener** interface has **getX()** and **getY()** methods, which return the current mouse coordinates relative to the component generating the event.

Mouse.java

1. Edit a copy of **Window.java** from page 135, changing the class name in the declaration, the constructor, and the instance statement from "Window" to "Mouse". Then, add an initial statement to import the functionality of the **java.awt.event** package

```
import java.awt.event.* ;
```

2. Edit the class declaration to add a **MouseListener** interface and **MouseMotionListener** interface to the program

```
class Mouse extends JFrame
        implements MouseListener , MouseMotionListener
```

3. Before the **Mouse()** constructor, create a **JTextArea** component and two integer variables to store coordinates

```
JTextArea txtArea = new JTextArea( 8 , 38 ) ;
int x , y ;
```

4. In the **Mouse()** constructor, insert statements to add the **JTextArea** component to the **JPanel** container and to make it generate **MouseEvent** events

```
pnl.add( txtArea ) ;
txtArea.addMouseMotionListener( this ) ;
txtArea.addMouseListener( this ) ;
```

5. After the constructor method, add the two event-handlers for the **MouseMotionListener** interface

```
public void mouseMoved( MouseEvent event )
{ x = event.getX() ; y = event.getY() ;    }
public void mouseDragged( MouseEvent event ) { }
```

6. Add five event-handlers for the **MouseListener** interface

```
public void mouseEntered( MouseEvent event )
{ txtArea.setText( "\nMouse Entered" ) ;            }

public void mousePressed( MouseEvent event )
{ txtArea.append( "\nMouse Pressed at X: " +x+ "Y: " +y ) ; }

public void mouseReleased( MouseEvent event )
{ txtArea.append( "\nMouse Released" ) ;            }

public void mouseClicked(MouseEvent event ) {  }
public void mouseExited(MouseEvent event )  {  }
```

7. Save the program as **Mouse.java**, then compile and run the program, clicking on the **JTextArea** component

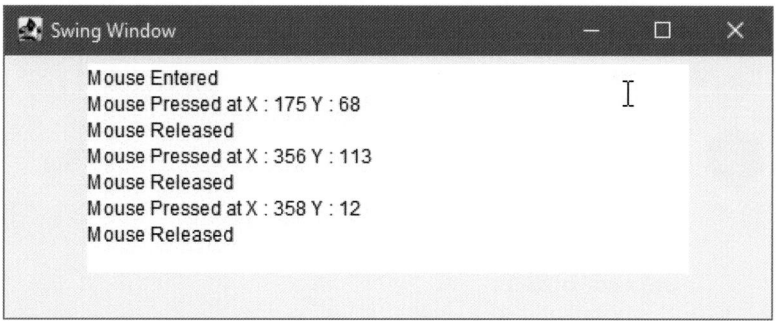

Rollover effects can be created by swapping images with the **mouseEntered()** and **mouseExited()** event-handler methods.

Announcing messages

The Swing **JOptionPane** class is designed to create a standard dialog box centered on its parent window. Its **showMessageDialog()** method displays a message to the user providing information, warning, or error description.

The **showMessageDialog()** method can take four arguments:

- Parent object – typically referenced by the **this** keyword
- Message **String** to be displayed
- Dialog title **String**
- One of the **JOptionPane** constants:

  INFORMATION_MESSAGE

  WARNING_MESSAGE or **ERROR_MESSAGE**

The dialog box will display an appropriate icon according to which **JOptionPane** constant is specified.

Messages.java

1. Edit a copy of **Window.java** from page 135, changing the class name in the declaration, the constructor, and the instance statement from "Window" to "Messages"

2. Add an initial statement to import the functionality of the **java.awt.event** package
```
import java.awt.event.* ;
```

3. Edit the class declaration to add an **ActionListener** interface to the program
```
class Messages extends JFrame implements ActionListener
```

4. Before the **Messages()** constructor, create three **JButton** components
```
JButton btn1= new JButton( "Show Information Message" ) ;
JButton btn2= new JButton( "Show Warning Message" ) ;
JButton btn3= new JButton( "Show Error Message" ) ;
```

5. Insert statements to add the button components to the **JPanel** container
```
pnl.add( btn1 ) ;
pnl.add( btn2 ) ;
pnl.add( btn3 ) ;
```

6. In the **Messages()** constructor, insert statements to make each button generate an **ActionEvent** event

```
btn1.addActionListener( this ) ;
btn2.addActionListener( this ) ;
btn3.addActionListener( this ) ;
```

7. After the constructor method, add an event-handler method for the **ActionListener** interface

```
public void actionPerformed( ActionEvent event ) {        }
```

8. Between the curly brackets of the event-handler, insert **if** statements to display a dialog when a button gets clicked

```
if ( event.getSource() == btn1 )
JOptionPane.showMessageDialog( this , "Information..." ,
"Message Dialog", JOptionPane.INFORMATION_MESSAGE ) ;

if ( event.getSource() == btn2 )
JOptionPane.showMessageDialog( this , "Warning..." ,
"Message Dialog" , JOptionPane.WARNING_MESSAGE ) ;

if ( event.getSource() == btn3 )
JOptionPane.showMessageDialog( this , "Error..." ,
"Message Dialog" , JOptionPane.ERROR_MESSAGE ) ;
```

9. Save the program as **Messages.java** then compile and run the program, clicking on each button

You can also simply specify the parent and message as two arguments to create a dialog with the default information icon and the default "Message" title.

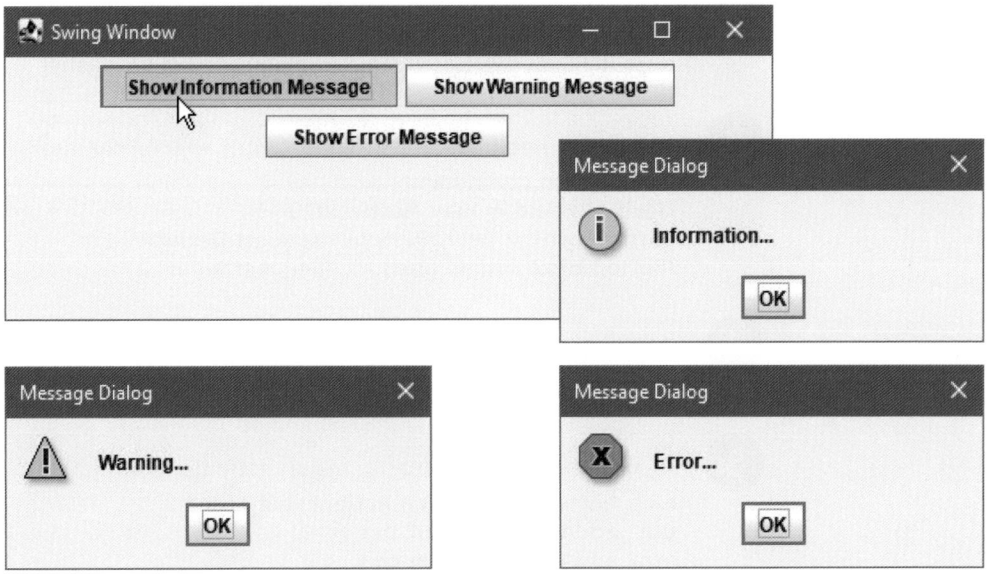

Requesting input

The Swing **JOptionPane** class can request information from the user by opening a dialog box with its **showConfirmationDialog()** method, requesting a decision, or with its **showInputDialog()** method, requesting user input.

Both these methods can take four arguments:

- Parent object – typically referenced by the **this** keyword
- Request **String** to be displayed
- Dialog title **String**
- One of the **JOptionPane** constants such as **PLAIN_MESSAGE** or to specify dialog decision buttons as **YES_NO_CANCEL_OPTION**

The dialog box will return the input **String** from an input dialog or an integer from a decision button – zero for yes, 1 for no, or 2 for cancel.

Request.java

1. Edit a copy of **Window.java** from page 135, changing the class name in the declaration, the constructor, and the instance statement from "Window" to "Request". Then, add an initial statement to import the functionality of the **java.awt.event** package
```
import java.awt.event.* ;
```

2. Edit the class declaration to add an **ActionListener** interface to the program
```
class Request extends JFrame implements ActionListener
```

3. Before the **Request()** constructor, create a **JTextField** and two **JButton** components
```
JTextField field = new JTextField( 38 ) ;
JButton btn1 = new JButton( "Request Decision" ) ;
JButton btn2 = new JButton( "Request Input" ) ;
```

4. Add each component to the **JPanel** container
```
pnl.add( field ) ; pnl.add( btn1 ) ; pnl.add( btn2 ) ;
```

5. In the **Request()** constructor, insert statements to make each button generate an **ActionEvent** event
```
btn1.addActionListener( this ) ;
btn2.addActionListener( this ) ;
```

6. After the constructor method, add an event-handler method for the **ActionListener** interface

```
public void actionPerformed( ActionEvent event ) {          }
```

7. Between the curly brackets of the event-handler, insert an **if** statement to respond to a decision button click

```
if ( event.getSource() == btn1 )
{
        int n = JOptionPane.showConfirmDialog( this ,
                "Do you agree?" , "Confirmation Dialog" ,
                JOptionPane.YES_NO_CANCEL_OPTION ) ;
        switch( n )
        {
                case 0 : field.setText( "Agreed" ) ; break ;
                case 1 : field.setText( "Disagreed" ) ; break ;
                case 2 : field.setText( "Canceled" ) ; break ;
        }
}
```

The **OK_CANCEL** constant provides two decision buttons – **OK** returns zero and **CANCEL** returns 2. Refer to the documentation for the full range of constants.

8. Insert an **if** statement to handle user input

```
if ( event.getSource() == btn2 )
field.setText( JOptionPane.showInputDialog( this ,
                "Enter your comment" , "Input Dialog" ,
                JOptionPane.PLAIN_MESSAGE ) ) ;
```

9. Save the program as **Request.java** then compile and run the program, clicking on each button

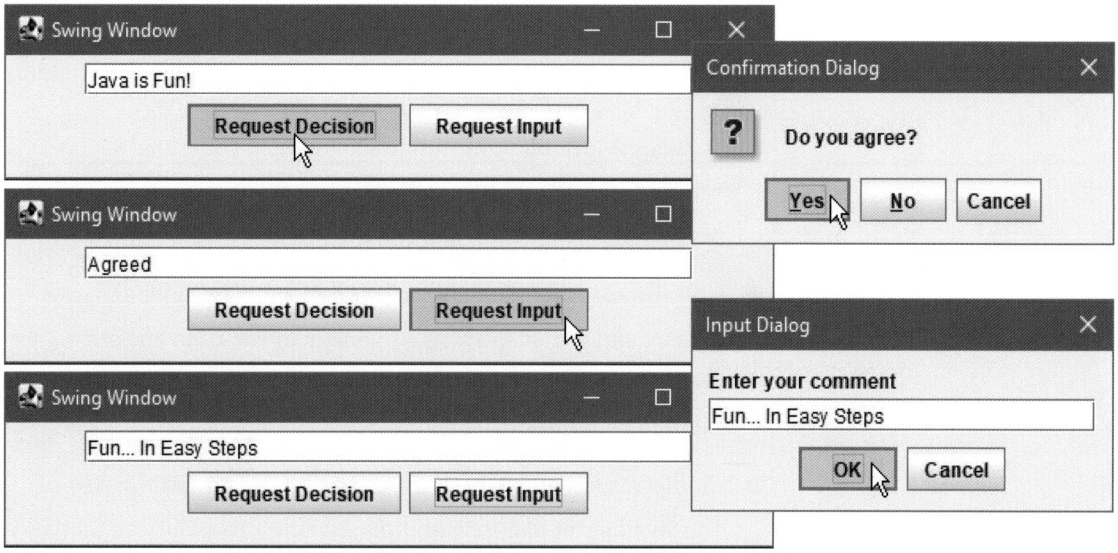

Summary

- The **implements** keyword can be used in a class declaration to add one or more **EventListener** interfaces.
- A component's **addActionListener()** method takes the **this** keyword as its argument – to make that component generate an **ActionEvent** event when it is activated.
- The **ActionListener** interface passes a generated **ActionEvent** event as the argument to its **actionPerformed()** event-handler, which can respond to a push button click made by the user.
- The **getSource()** method of an **ActionEvent** event can be used to identify the originating component that generated the event.
- An **ItemListener** interface passes a generated **ItemEvent** event as the argument to its **itemStateChanged()** event-handler, which can respond to an item selection made by the user.
- The **getItemSelectable()** method of an **ItemEvent** event can be used to identify the component that generated the event.
- A **KeyListener** interface passes a generated **KeyEvent** event as the argument to three required event-handler methods, which can respond to a key press and reveal that key's character.
- A **MouseListener** interface passes a generated **MouseEvent** event as the argument to five required event-handler methods, which can respond to mouse actions made by the user.
- A **MouseMotionListener** interface passes a generated **MouseEvent** event as the argument to two required event-handlers, which can respond to mouse movement.
- The **showMessageDialog()** method of the **JOptionPane** class creates a dialog displaying a message to the user, and its **showInputDialog()** and **showConfirmationDialog()** methods can be used to request user input.
- Audio resources can be represented by the **AudioClip** class of the **java.applet** package, and played using its **play()** method.

10 Deploying programs

This chapter demonstrates how to deploy Java programs – both as Java archives (JAR) and Android application packages (APK).

168 Producing an application

170 Distributing programs

172 Building Java archives

173 Deploying applications

174 Creating Android projects

176 Exploring project files

178 Adding resources & controls

180 Inserting Java code

182 Testing the application

184 Deploying Android apps

186 Summary

Producing an application

Java applications for both desktop and handheld devices can be created from common code – like the **Lotto.java** program below:

Lotto.java

```
import javax.swing.* ;
import java.awt.event.* ;

public class Lotto extends JFrame implements ActionListener
{
  ClassLoader ldr = this.getClass( ).getClassLoader( ) ;
  java.net.URL iconURL = ldr.getResource( "Lotto.png" ) ;
  ImageIcon icon = new ImageIcon( iconURL ) ;
  JLabel img = new JLabel( icon ) ;
  JTextField txt = new JTextField( "" , 18 ) ;
  JButton btn = new JButton( "Get My Lucky Numbers" ) ;
  JPanel pnl = new JPanel( ) ;

  public Lotto( )
  {
     super( "Lotto App" ) ; setSize( 260 , 210 ) ;
     setDefaultCloseOperation( JFrame.EXIT_ON_CLOSE ) ;
     pnl.add( img ) ; pnl.add( txt ) ; pnl.add( btn ) ;
     btn.addActionListener( this ) ; add( pnl ) ; setVisible( true ) ;
  }

  public void actionPerformed( ActionEvent event )
  {
     if ( event.getSource( ) == btn )
     {
        int[ ] nums = new int[ 60 ] ; String str = "" ;
        for ( int i = 1 ; i < 60 ; i++ ) { nums[ i ] = i ; }
        for ( int i = 1 ; i < 60 ; i++ )
        {       int r= ( int ) ( 59 * Math.random( ) ) + 1 ;
                int t= nums[ i ] ; nums[ i ]= nums[ r ] ; nums[ r ]= t ;
        }
        for ( int i = 1 ; i < 7 ; i++ )
        {       str += " " + Integer.toString( nums[ i ] ) + " " ;  }
        txt.setText( str ) ;
     }
  }

  public static void main ( String[ ] args )
  {  Lotto lotto = new Lotto( ) ;          }
}
```

Components → `JLabel img = new JLabel( icon ) ;`

Constructor → `public Lotto( )`

Event-handler → `public void actionPerformed( ActionEvent event )`

Entry-point → `public static void main ( String[ ] args )`

The algorithm in this event-handler shuffles integers 1-59 in an array, then assigns those integers in the first six elements to a string.

The Lotto program begins with import statements to make Swing components and the **ActionListener** interface available.

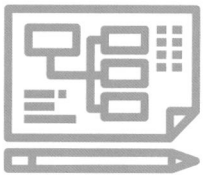

Components

The program comprises a single panel component containing a label component to display an image, a text field component to display output, and a button component for user interaction.

Constructor

The **Lotto( )** constructor builds a simple Swing interface that loads the panel into a window frame measuring 260 x 210.

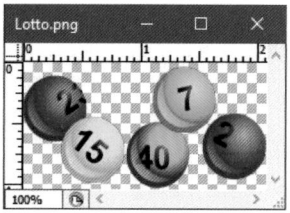

Lotto.png – Checkered areas are transparent.

Event-handler

The button's event-handler method executes an algorithm to select a sequence of six unique random numbers in the range of 1-59 for display in the text field component.

Entry-point

The **main( )** method creates an instance of the app, and calls upon **ClassLoader( )** to seek the image file resource **Lotto.png** in the same directory as the program file. The files must be arranged in this way before attempting to compile the program.

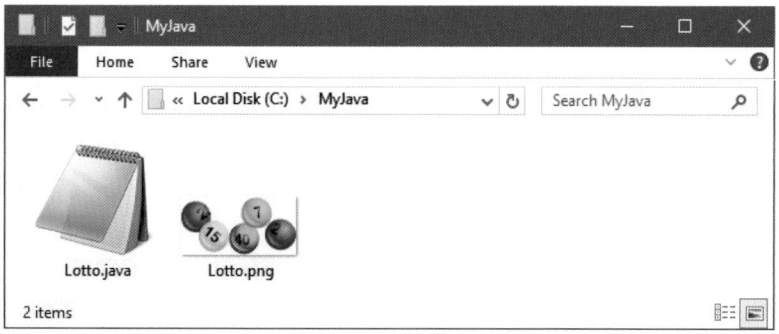

The Lotto program is used throughout this chapter to create apps for desktop and handheld devices.

Observing the required file arrangement, the **javac** compiler can be employed in the usual way to create a **Lotto.class** file, then the **java** interpreter can be employed to execute the program:

Distributing programs

The **Lotto** program opens a new window of the specified size containing the Swing interface components. Each time the user clicks the push button, its event-handler displays six new random numbers in the range 1-59 within the text field component:

The **.java** source code file need not be included when distributing a program – only **.class** and resource files are needed.

As with other examples in this book, the **Lotto** program has been compiled here for Java and can be distributed for execution on other computers where an appropriate Java Runtime Environment (JRE) is present – regardless of their operating system. For example, in the screenshots below, **Lotto.class** and **Lotto.png** files have been copied to the desktop of a computer running the Linux operating system with the Java runtime installed. The **Lotto** program can, therefore, be executed by the **java** interpreter in the same way as on the originating Windows system.

There is, however, a danger in distributing Java programs this way as the program will fail to execute if resource files become unavailable – in this case, removing **Lotto.png** produces this error:

```
Terminal
File  Edit  View  Search  Terminal  Help
mike ▸ java Lotto
Exception in thread "main" java.lang.NullPointerException
        at java.desktop/javax.swing.ImageIcon.<init>(ImageIcon.java:217)
        at Lotto.<init>(Lotto.java:9)
        at Lotto.main(Lotto.java:61)
mike ▸
```

The JDK contains a **jar** utility tool that allows program class and resource files to be bundled into a single Java ARchive (JAR) file. This compresses all program files, using the popular ZIP format, into a single file with a **.jar** file extension. A JAR file stores the program efficiently and helps ensure that resource files do not become accidentally isolated. The **java** interpreter fully supports JAR files so Java applications can be executed without extracting the individual files. Like the **java** interpreter and **javac** compiler, the **jar** tool is located in Java's **bin** directory and runs from the command line to perform these common **jar** operations:

Command syntax:	Operation:
jar cf ***jar-file input-file/s***	Create a JAR file
jar cfe ***jar-file entry-point input-file/s***	Create a JAR file with a specified entry point in a stand-alone application
jar tf ***jar-file***	View contents of a JAR file
jar uf ***jar-file***	Update contents of JAR file
jar ufm ***jar-file attribute-file***	Update contents of JAR file manifest, adding attribute/s
jar xf ***jar-file***	Extract all contents of JAR
jar xf ***jar-file archived-file/s***	Extract specific files from JAR

Larger programs may use many resource files whose location can easily be disrupted by a user – the solution is to package the program and all its resources into a single executable archive file.

For larger programs, the * wildcard character can be used to archive multiple files within the directory – for instance, **jar cf Program.jar *.class** archives all class files in the current directory.

Building Java archives

Follow these steps to create a JAR file for the Lotto program described at the start of this chapter:

Lotto.jar

1. Open a command-line/terminal window, then navigate to the directory where the Lotto program files are located – **Lotto.class** and **Lotto.png**

2. Enter **jar cfe Lotto.jar Lotto Lotto.class Lotto.png**, then hit the **Enter** key to create a **Lotto.jar** archive

3. Next, enter **jar tf Lotto.jar** to see all contents of the JAR

```
Command Prompt

C:\MyJava> jar cfe Lotto.jar Lotto Lotto.class Lotto.png

C:\MyJava> jar tf Lotto.jar
META-INF/
META-INF/MANIFEST.MF
Lotto.class
Lotto.png

C:\MyJava>
```

Notice that the **jar** tool automatically creates a **META-INF** directory alongside the archived files. This contains a text-based manifest meta file named **MANIFEST.MF** that you can examine:

The JAR manifest can be modified for advanced purposes, such as the addition of permissions to use system resources.

4. Now, enter **jar xf Lotto.jar META-INF** to extract a copy of the **META-INF** directory

5. Finally, enter **type META-INF\MANIFEST.MF** to see the text contained within the archive manifest

```
Command Prompt

C:\MyJava> jar xf Lotto.jar META-INF

C:\MyJava> type META-INF\MANIFEST.MF
Manifest-Version: 1.0
Created-By: XX.X.X (AdoptOpenJDK)
Main-Class: Lotto


C:\MyJava>
```

Deploying applications

Java JAR files are executable on any system on which the appropriate version of the Java Runtime is installed:

1. At the command line, navigate to the directory where the **Lotto.jar** file is located, then type **java -jar Lotto.jar** and hit the **Enter** key to run the Lotto application

The **.jar** file extension is required when executing JAR files from a prompt.

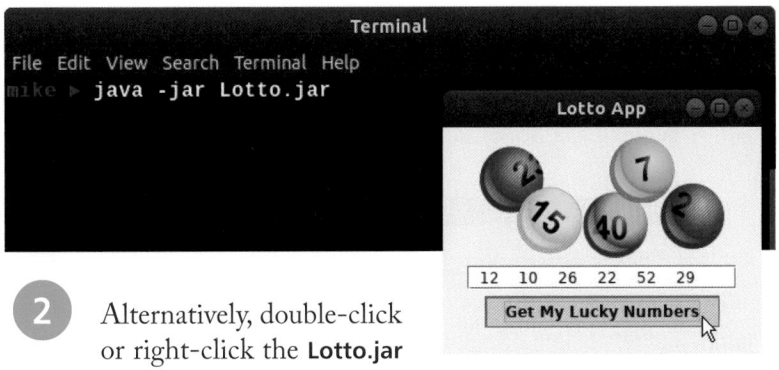

2. Alternatively, double-click or right-click the **Lotto.jar** file icon, and choose to "Open With" the Java Runtime

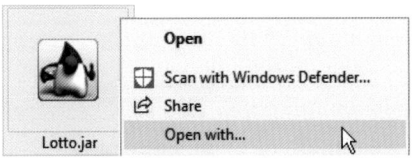

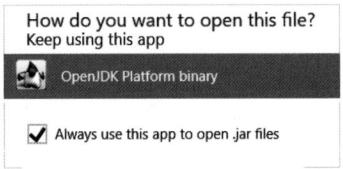

Set the JRE as the default JAR file handler on your system for permanent double-click execution.

Creating Android projects

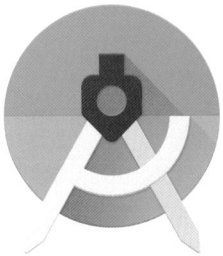

Android Studio is available free from **developer.android.com/studio**
This chapter describes Android application development using the latest version of Android Studio available at the time of writing – instructions may vary for other versions.

The Android operating system, prevalent on handheld devices, includes a set of core libraries that provide most of the functionality of those in the Java programming language. This means that Java programs can be readily converted for Android.

Android app development is best undertaken using the official Android Studio Integrated Development Environment (IDE). This provides a unified environment where you can develop apps for all Android devices, and provides extensive testing tools. Completed apps are distributed as an Android Application Package (APK) archive file, which is similar to a Java archive (JAR) file. This compresses all program files, using the popular ZIP format, into a single file with a **.apk** file extension. Each app is first created in Android Studio as a "project", to which the developer adds code and resources:

1. Launch Android Studio, then choose to **Start a new Android Studio project** in the "Welcome" dialog options – to open the "Choose your project" dialog

2. Select the target device type and the type of activity – typically "Phone and Tablet" and "Empty Activity"

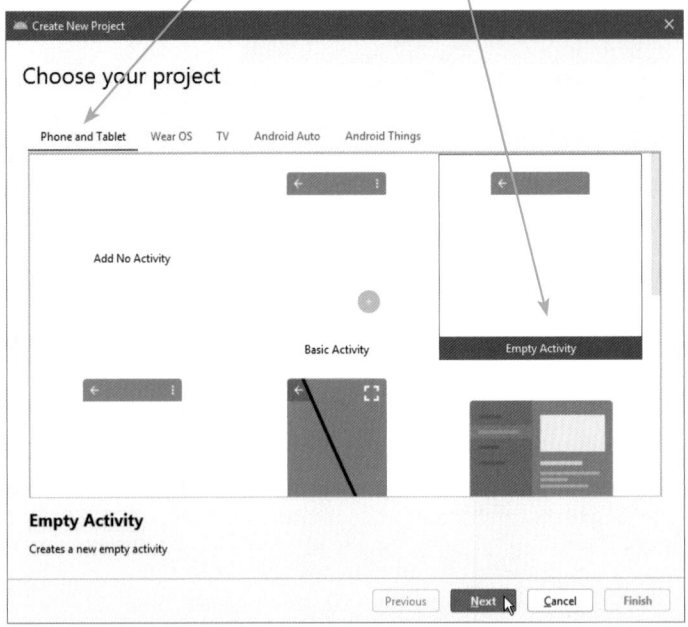

3. Click **Next** to open the "Configure your project" dialog

4. Enter a project **Name**, for example, "Lotto"

5. Enter a **Package name** as **com.*domain.appname***

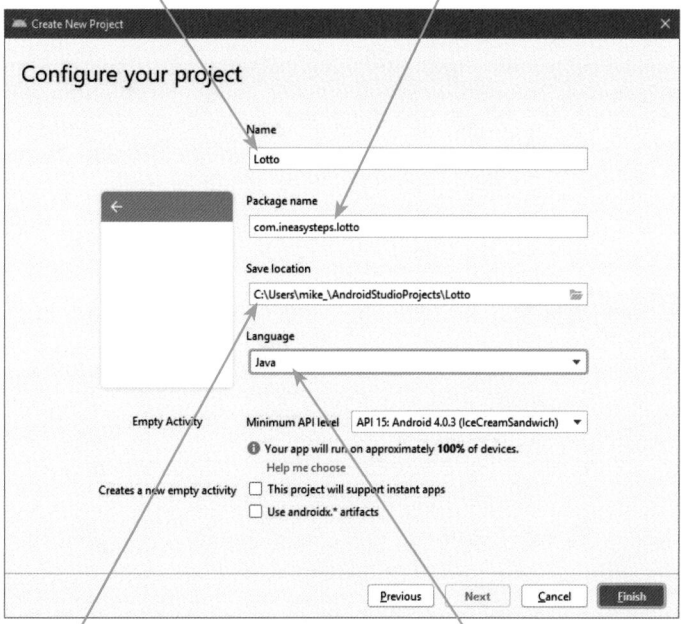

6. Choose a preferred **Save location** on your computer

7. Set the coding **Language** to "Java"

8. Choose the **Minimum API level** a device will need to run the app ("Ice Cream Sandwich" is the default)

9. Click the **Finish** button to create an Android project using your specified configuration

10. Wait while Android Studio now generates several files and folders for the new project (this can take a while), then eventually you will see the IDE interface appear

Choose API 15 if you would like the app to run on 100% of devices active on the Google Play Store.

Exploring project files

The Android Studio IDE provides a Project window that displays an expandable tree view of all files and folders within the project.

You can click any arrow in the Project window to expand a folder, and double-click on any file in the Project window to open it in the tabbed Editor window.

Lotto [C:\Users\mike_\AndroidStudioProjects\Lotto]

File Edit View Navigate Code Analyze Refactor Build Run Tools VCS Window Help

java > com > ineasysteps > lotto > MainActivity

app

Android

- app
  - manifests
  - java
    - com.ineasysteps.lotto
      - MainActivity
    - com.ineasysteps.lotto (androidTest)
    - com.ineasysteps.lotto (test)
  - res
    - drawable
    - layout
      - activity_main.xml
    - mipmap
    - values
- Gradle Scripts

activity_main.xml | MainActivity.java

```
1   package com.ineasysteps.lotto;
2
3   import android.support.v7.app.AppCompatActivity;
4   import android.os.Bundle;
5
6   public class MainActivity extends AppCompatActivity {
7
8       @Override
9       protected void onCreate(Bundle savedInstanceState) {
10          super.onCreate(savedInstanceState);
11          setContentView(R.layout.activity_main);
12      }
13  }
14
```

1: Project | Resource Manager | Build Variants | Gradle | Device File Explorer

TODO | Terminal | Build | 6: Logcat | Event Log

1:1 CRLF ÷ UTF-8 ÷ 4 spaces ÷

Project window

Editor window

If the Project window is not immediately visible, click the Project button in the left sidebar, or open it using the shortcut keys Alt + F1.

Despite its initial appearance of complexity, only two files need modification by the developer to create a customized application:

- **MainActivity.java** – the Java file that loads controls into the app interface and can contain event-handler code to respond to user actions within the app interface.
- **activity_main.xml** – the XML file that defines each control to appear in the app interface and their layout.

Selecting the **activity_main.xml** file in the Project window presents it in the Editor window in one of two possible views – visually in Design view or programmatically in Text view. There are tabs at the bottom of the window to switch between views.

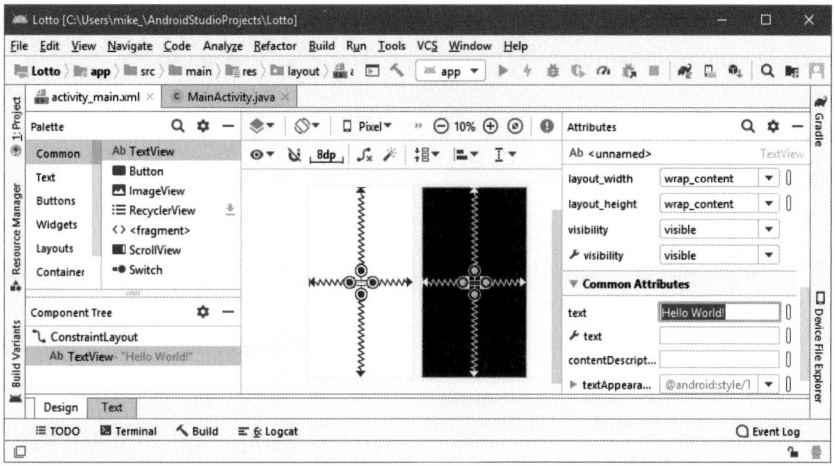

Design view provides a Palette of controls that can be dragged onto a graphical representation of the app, a Component Tree to select any added control, and an Attributes window in which to modify the appearance of a selected control.

Text view provides a "code-behind" version of the layout that describes each aspect of added controls using XML attributes.

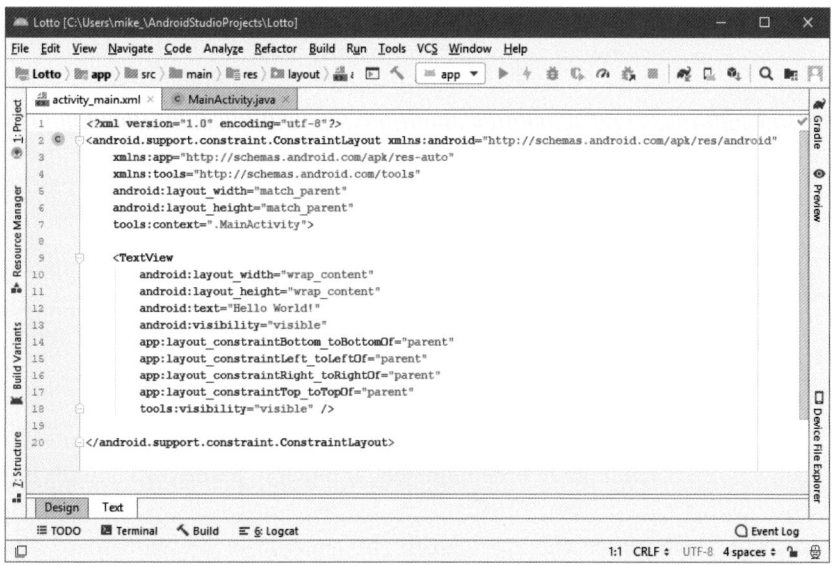

Controls can be added to the app interface and modified either visually in Design view or programmatically in Text view.

Adding resources & controls

Image resources

To begin customizing the default Android Studio empty app for the Lotto program, the image can first be added as a "resource":

1. Right-click on the **Lotto.png** image, and choose **Copy**

2. Next, right-click on the **app>res>drawable** folder in the Project window, and choose **Paste**

3. Choose a Destination Directory, then rename the file to lowercase as **lotto.png**

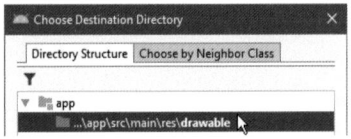

4. Click **OK** to see the file now appear in the **drawable** folder

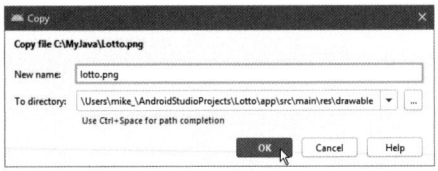

Android only supports lowercase filenames for resource items.

Interface controls

The Lotto app will require three interface controls in a vertical layout – an ImageView control for the logo, a TextView control for the output, and a Button control for user interaction:

activity_main.xml

1. Open the **activity_main.xml** file in the Editor's Text view

2. Insert this ImageView control element immediately before the existing default TextView element

```
<ImageView
  android:layout_width="match_parent"
  android:layout_height="wrap_content"
  app:srcCompat="@drawable/lotto"
  android:id="@+id/imageView"
  android:contentDescription="Lotto Logo
  app:layout_constraintTop_toTopOf="parent" />
```

The **app:srcCompat** attribute references the image resource added to the **drawable** folder.

The attributes in this element fit the control to the width of the layout container, and position the control at the top of the container. The image resource is defined as the content source, and the element is given an id for reference by other elements.

3. Edit the existing TextView element to look like this:

```
<TextView
  android:layout_width="match_parent"
  android:layout_height="wrap_content"
  android:id="@+id/textView
  android:height="60dp"
  android:textSize="36sp"
  android:gravity="center_horizontal"
  app:layout_constraintTop_toBottomOf =
                                "@+id/imageView" />
```

The **android:id** attribute in each element specifies a unique name by which the element can be referenced in Java code.

4. Insert this element right after the TextView element

```
<Button
  android:layout_width="match_parent"
  android:layout_height="wrap_content"
  android:id="@+id/button"
  android:textSize="24sp"
  android:onClick="lotto"
  android:text="GET MY LUCKY NUMBERS"
  app:layout_constraintTop_toBottomOf =
                                "@+id/textView" />
```

The **android:onClick** attribute specifies the name of an event-handler to be called.

String resources

The strings assigned to describe the image content and to specify the button text should each be converted to a string resource:

1. Click within the **"Lotto Logo"** string assignment to give it focus, then press **Alt** + **Enter** to see a QuickFix dialog

```
android:contentDescription="Lotto Logo"
```

Extract string resource
Suppress: Add tools:ignore="HardcodedText" attribute

2. Choose **Extract string resource**, then provide a resource name in the "Extract Resource" dialog that now appears

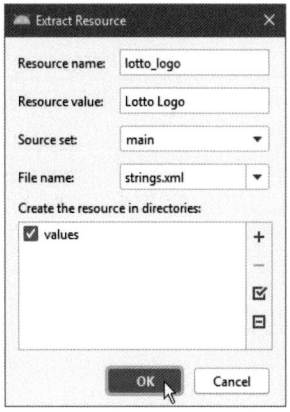

3. Click **OK** to close the dialog, and see the assigned string get replaced by a reference to the new string resource

```
android:contentDescription="@string/lotto_logo"
```

4. Repeat this for the **"GET MY LUCKY NUMBERS"** string

```
android:text="@string/get_my_lucky_numbers"
```

Inserting Java code

After adding resources and controls shown on page 179, the app interface should now resemble that of the **Lotto.jar** application:

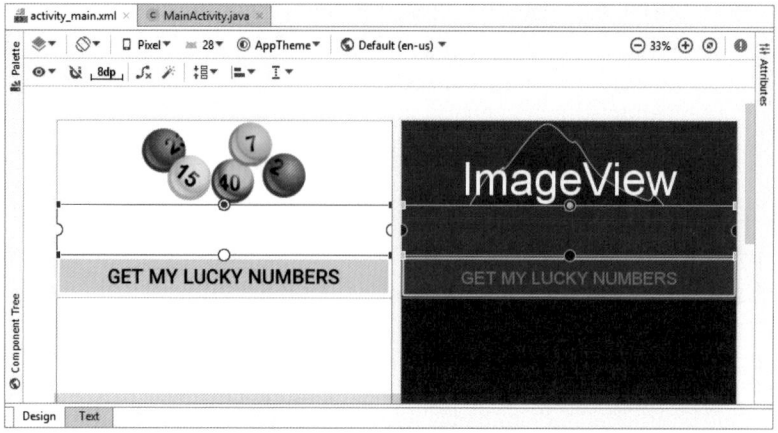

If the controls do not look like this screenshot, you should return to page 179 and carefully check each element's attributes.

Functionality can next be added to the app by inserting an event-handler into the **MainActivity.java** file that will respond to the button's **onClick** event when the user pushes the button. This event automatically passes one argument to the event-handler, which is an identifying reference to the control that has been clicked. Consequently, the event-handler signature must accommodate the argument by including a parameter for the **View** class – the base class of all widgets. The method must also have a **void** return type:

MainActivity.java

1. First add this line to the import statements at the beginning of the **MainActivity.java** file
   import android.view.View ;

2. Insert this event-handler signature into the **MainActivity** class, immediately after its **onCreate( )** method block
   public void lotto(View vue) { }

Interface controls can be referenced in code by specifying their identity as the argument to a **findViewById( )** method. This is the name assigned to their **android:id** attribute in **activity_main.xml** prefixed by **R.id.** :

3. Inside the event-handler block, assign a reference to the **<TextView>** control element to a variable
   TextView txt = (TextView) findViewById(R.id.textView) ;

4. Finally, inside the event-handler block, copy the code from the event-handler in the **Lotto.java** program (listed on page 168) that outputs six unique random numbers

```
int[ ] nums = new int[ 60 ] ; String str = " " ;
for ( int i = 1 ; i < 60 ; i++ ) { nums[ i ] = i ; }
for ( int i = 1 ; i < 60 ; i++ )
{
  int r= ( int ) ( 59 * Math.random( ) ) + 1 ;
  int t= nums[ i ] ; nums[ i ]= nums[ r ] ; nums[ r ]= t ;
}
for ( int i = 1 ; i < 7 ; i++ )
{str += " " + Integer.toString( nums[ i ] ) + " " ; }
txt.setText( str ) ;
```

In this case, there is no need for the code to check the source of the call, as the event-handler is explicitly assigned to the button by the **android:onClick** attribute in **activity_main.xml**.

Now that the Lotto app has all resources, controls, and functional code in place, an attempt can be made to build the project:

5. On the Android Studio main toolbar, click **View**, **Tool Windows**, **Build** – to open the "Build" window

6. Then, click **Build**, **Make Project** (or press the **Ctrl** + **F9** shortcut) to start building – see its progress displayed in the "Build" window

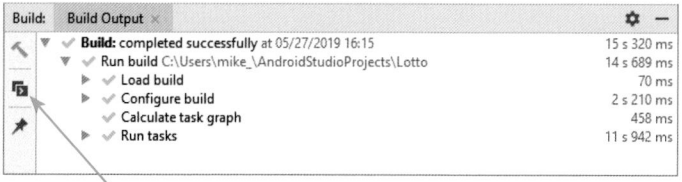

7. Click the "Toggle View" button to see a confirmation of build success, or failure

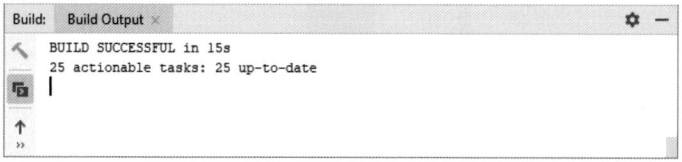

8. Fix any reported errors if necessary, then build again until you see a confirmation of success

If the build attempt fails, look for red light bulb icons in the code – Android Studio adds these so you can easily find and correct errors.

Testing the application

Once an application project has built successfully, it is ready to be tested. Testing can be performed on a real Android device, connected to your computer via a USB socket, or on an Android Virtual Device (AVD) emulator. AVDs allow you to test how the app will perform on a range of devices, but they do use more system resources and can be painfully slow. Applications should be tested on at least one phone device and one tablet device:

Creation of each AVD emulator may require a large system image file to be downloaded. You may prefer to test on a real Android device. Also note that accelerated emulators will only run if your computer has a CPU that supports hardware virtualization (Intel VT-x or AMD SVM).

1. Click **Run, Run 'app'** (or press the **Shift + F10** shortcut) to open the "Select Deployment Target" dialog

2. Select an AVD phone emulator to connect, then click **OK** to install the Lotto app on the emulator

3. Push the app's button to see the TextView content unhappily wrap on this small device screen

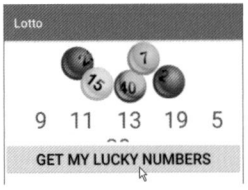

4. Edit **activity_main.xml** to reduce the text size **android:textSize="26sp"**

5. Click **Build, Rebuild Project** to apply the change, then run the app in the emulator once more to see the solution

It is better to test on real devices rather than the emulators. Ideally, you should test on as many different devices as possible before final deployment of apps.

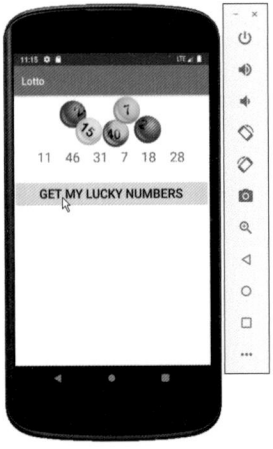

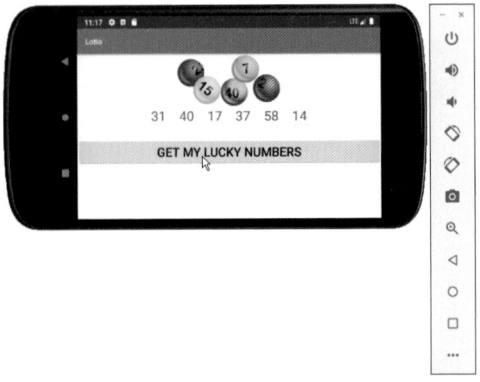

Android Studio has an Instant Run feature that automatically updates changes to the app so they appear in the test device more quickly.

6. Take an Android phone and enable "USB Debugging" in the **Settings, Developer Options** menu

7. Connect the phone to your computer via a USB port, and tap to allow access

8. Click **Run, Run 'app'** (or press the **Shift** + **F10** shortcut) to open the "Select Deployment Target" dialog

9. Select the connected phone device, then click **OK** to install the Lotto app onto the phone

10. Push the app's button to see the Lotto app happily perform as expected – a successful test

The test processes provide an application launcher so the tablet can be disconnected and the app launched by tapping the launcher icon – but remember, this is a Debug build of the app.

If you cannot see Developer Options in the Android Settings you can enable it by tapping on the Build Number seven times – typically found at Settings, About, Software Information, Build Number.

Android Studio provides a default image launcher icon, but you can use your own image. In the Project window, right-click on the **res** folder then choose **New**, **Image Asset** to open the Asset Studio, then select **Image** and browse to an image you wish to import into the project.

Deploying Android apps

After successful testing, the development Debug version of an app should be changed to a Release version before deployment as an Android Application Package (APK). Android requires that all APKs must be digitally signed with a certificate, and Android Studio allows you to easily generate a signed APK:

1. Click **Build**, **Generate Signed Bundle/ APK** on the Android Studio menu

2. Select the **APK** option, then click the **Next** button

Choose the Android App Bundle option if you want to upload the app to the Google Play store.

3. Enter your existing key store details, or click the **Create new...** button to create a key store

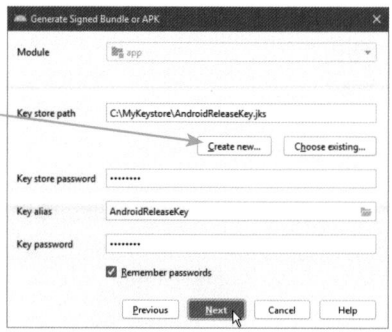

4. Enter the key store passwords, then click the **Next** button

A key store holds public/ private key pairs. You, as the owner, retain the private key, while the Android Studio signing tool attaches the public key to the APK. This uniquely associates the APK to ensure that any future updates to the APK come from you: the original developer.

5. Select the **release** option

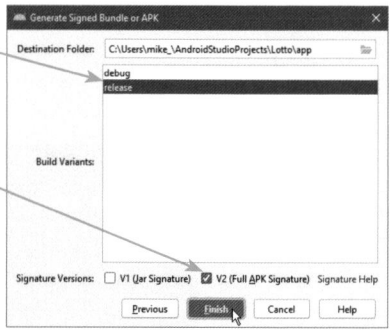

6. Check the **V2** signature version

7. Click **Finish** to generate a signed APK for the app

8. Find the generated APK by clicking **locate** on the notification that appears, then rename the APK from **app-release.apk** to **Lotto.apk**

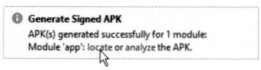

Installation of APKs from sources other than Google Play is blocked unless the user opts to allow them:

1. Download **Lotto.apk** to an Android device, then tap the file icon to attempt installation

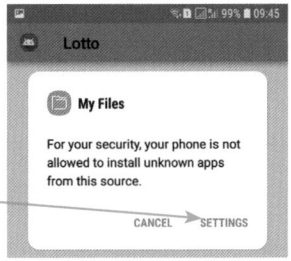

2. Select the **SETTINGS** option on the security dialog

3. Slide the control to the ON position for the option to **Allow from this source**, then click **Install** when asked

4. Now select the **INSTALL ANYWAY** option on the Play Protect dialog

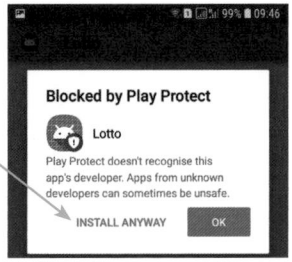

5. Wait while the app gets installed onto the device

On earlier versions of Android go to Settings, Security and opt to "Allow installation of apps from unknown sources".

Play Protect is a security safeguard built into every device with Google Play.

Summary

- Java programs can be deployed as stand-alone desktop applications running on an appropriate version of the JRE.
- Application files can be distributed for execution on other operating systems using the appropriate **java** interpreter.
- Bundling all program files into a single JAR archive file helps ensure resource files do not become accidentally isolated.
- Executable JAR applications can be executed from a prompt with the **java -jar** command or by clicking on their file icon.
- Java programs can be readily converted for the Android operating system as it includes similar core libraries.
- Android Studio is the official IDE for the development of Android applications.
- APK and JAR archive files are both compressed in ZIP format.
- Each Android app is first created as a project to which the developer adds code and resources.
- The most used windows in the Android Studio interface are the Project window and the Editor window.
- Functional code can be added to the **MainActivity.java** file and interface components added to the **activity_main.xml** file.
- An Android app can store images and strings as resources.
- The signature of a button's **onClick** event-handler must include a parameter for a **View** class object.
- Interface components can be referenced in code by specifying their identity as the argument to **findViewById( )**.
- Android Studio provides AVD emulators for testing, and also allows testing to be performed on real connected devices.
- The Release version of an Android app must be digitally signed with a public key certificate.

Index

A

Abstract Window Toolkit 146
Access modifier 102
ActionListener. *See* EventListener interfaces
ActionListener interface 169
activity_main.xml file 176
Addition operator, + 26
AdoptOpenJDK 9
AND bitwise operator, & 40
AND operator, && 32, 45
Android Application Package (APK) 174, 184
Android Studio 174, 176
Android Virtual Device (AVD) emulator 182
Archiver, jar command 171
Arguments 66
Arithmetic operators
  +, -, *, /, % 26
ArrayList. *See* Classes
Arrays 64
  dimensions 74
  length 74
  sorting 124
Arrays class. *See* Classes
ASCII code values 62, 90
Assignment operators
  =, +=, -=, *=, /=, %= 28
Attributes 106
Attributes window 177

B

Behaviors 106
Bitwise operators
  &, |, ^, ~, <<, >> 40
Boolean data type, boolean 18
Boolean values 44, 50
Box container 149
  createVerticalBox() method 149
Branching statements
  else 46
  if 44
  switch 48
Break keyword, break 56
BufferedReader class. *See* Classes
BufferedWriter class. *See* Classes
Build Android project: 181
Button component, JButton 136
ButtonGroup class. *See* Classes
Byte data type, byte 18

C

Camel case naming convention 17
Case keyword, case 48
Casting data types 62
Catch keyword, catch 76
Certificate 184
Character data type, char 18
Checkbox component, JCheckBox 142
Class attributes and behaviors 106
Class declaration 13
Classes
  ActionEvent class
    getActionCommand() method 154
    getSource() method 153
  ArrayList class
    add() method 126
    get() method 126
    remove() method 126
    set() method 126
  Arrays class
    sort() method 124
  BufferedReader class
    readLine() method 118
  BufferedWriter class 122
  ButtonGroup class 144
  ClassLoader class 169
    getResource() method 137
  Color class
    setBackground() method 148
    setForeground() method 148
  Container class
    getContentPane() method 147
  Creating classes 102
  DateTimeFormatter class
    ofPattern() method 130
  Encapsulating properties 110
  File class
    createNewFile() method 116
    delete() method 116
    exists() method 116
    getName() method 116
    length() method 116
    list() method 116
    renameTo() method 116

FileReader class 120
FileWriter class
  newline() method 122
  write() method 122
FlowLayout class 134
ImageIcon class 136
InputStreamReader class 118
ItemEvent class
  getItemSelectable() method 156
  getStateChange() method 156
JButton class 136
  addActionListener() method 153
  setEnabled() method 154
JCheckBox class 142
JComboBox class 142
JFrame class
  add() method 134
  setDefaultCloseOperation() method 134
  setSize() method 134
  setVisible() method 134
  super() method 134
JLabel class
  setHorizontalPosition() method 138
  setOpaque() method 148
  setToolTipText() method 138
  setVerticalPosition() method 138
JList class 142
JOptionPane class
  showConfirmationDialog() method 164
  showInputDialog() method 164
  showMessageDialog() method 162
JPanel class 134
  add() method 136
JRadioButton class 144
JScrollPane class
  setHorizontalScrollBarPolicy() method 140
  setVerticalScrollBarPolicy() method 140
JTextArea class
  setLineWrap() method 140
  setWrapStyleWord() method 140
JTextField class 140
KeyEvent class
  getKeyChar() method 158
  getKeyCode() method 158
  getKeyText() method 158
LocalDateTime class
  getYear() method 128
  now() method 128
  withYear() method 128
Math class
  ceil() method 84
  E constant 82
  floor() method 84
  PI constant 82
  random() method 86
  round() method 84
MouseEvent class
  getX() method 160
  getY() method 160
NumberFormat class
  format() method 130
  getCurrencyInstance() method 130
  getNumberInstance() method 130
  getPerCentInstance() method 130
String class
  charAt() method 94
  endsWith() method 92
  equals() method 90
  indexOf() method 92
  length() method 88
  replace() method 94
  startsWith() method 92
  substring() method 92
  toLowerCase() method 90
  toUpperCase() method 90
  trim() method 94
System class
  in field 118
  out field println() method 80
URL class 137
Class methods 101
Class variables 101
Collection lists 126
Color on components 148
Command Prompt window 11
Comments
  Multiple line, /* */ 21
  Single line, // 21
Comparison operators
  ==, !=, >, >=, <, <= 30
compiler 14
Compiler
  errors 22
  javac command 9, 14
Complex expressions 45
  operator precedence 36
Component Tree 177
Conditional operator, ? : 34
Constants 20
Constructor method 108, 112
Continue keyword, continue 57
Creating a window 134

D

Data types 18
  boolean 18
  byte 18
  char 18
  double 18
  float 18
  int 18
  long 18
  short 18
  String 18
Date 128
  Formatter 130
Dates and times 128
Debug version 183-184
Decrement operator, -- 26
Default keyword, default 48
Deploying Android apps 184
Deploying applications 173
Design view 176-177
Dialog boxes 162
Division operator, / 26
Documentation 80
Do keyword, do 54
Dot notation 90
Double data type, double 18

E

EclipseAdoptium 9
Editor window 176
Elements 64
Else keyword, else 46
Enabling components 154
Encapsulation 110
Equality operator, == 30
Error
  handling 76
  resolution 22
Escape sequences
  \n, \t, \b, \r, \f, \\, \', \", 38
event-handler signature
  View class 180
EventListener interfaces
  ActionListener
    actionPerfomed() event-handler method 153
  ItemListener
    itemStateChanged() event-handler method 156
  KeyListener
    keyPressed() event-handler method 158
    keyReleased() event-handler method 158
    keyTyped() event-handler method 158
  MouseListener
    mouseClicked() event-handler method 160
    mouseEntered() event-handler method 160
    mouseExited() event-handler method 160
    mousePressed() event-handler method 160
    mouseReleased() event-handler method 160
  MouseMotionListener
    mouseDragged() event-handler method 160
    mouseMoved() event-handler method 160
Exception class 76
  ArrayIndexOutOfBoundsException 76
  IOException 120
  NumberFormatException 76
Exception handling 76
Extends keyword, extends 104, 134

F

False keyword, false 44
File class. *See* Classes
File extension
  .class 8
  .java 8
FileReader class. *See* Classes
FileWriter class. *See* Classes
Final keyword, final 20
Finally keyword, finally 76
Floating point data type, double 18
Floating point data type, float 18
Float.parseFloat() method 62
FlowLayout class. *See* Classes
Font on components 148
For keyword, for 50
Formatting numbers and dates 130

G

Generating events 153
Generating random numbers 86
Generic type <String> 126
Graphical user interface (GUI) 134
Greater than operator, > 30
Greater than or equal operator, >= 30

H

Hardware virtualization (Intel VT-x or AMD SVM) 182
Hello World program 12

I

If keyword, if 44
Image resources 178
Implements keyword, implements 152
Import keyword, import 116
Increment operator, ++ 26
Inequality operator, != 30
Inheritance 104, 108
Initializer 50
Input dialogs 164
InputStreamReader class. *See* Classes
Installation JDK 10
Instance methods 109
Instances 106
Instance variables 109
Integer data type, int 18
Integer.parseInt() method 62, 66
Integrated Development Environment (IDE) 174
Interpreter, java command 8, 15
ItemListener. *See* EventListener interfaces
Item selectors 142, 156

J

jar utility tool 171
Java API (Application Programming Interface) 80
Java archive (JAR) 137, 171
Java compiler, javac 8, 14
Java Development Kit (JDK) 9-10
Java interpreter, java 8
Java keywords 16
Java programming language 8
Java Runtime Environment (JRE) 9
Java SE (Standard Edition) 9
Java shell, jshell 11
Java Virtual Machine (Java VM) 8

K

Keyboard events 158
Key store 184
Keywords 16
- boolean 18
- break 56
- byte 18
- case 48
- catch 76
- char 18
- continue 57
- default 48
- do 54
- double 18
- else 46
- extends 104, 134
- false 44
- final 20
- finally 76
- float 18
- for 50
- if 44
- implements 152
- import 116
- int 18
- long 18
- new 64, 108
- null 88
- private 110
- public 102
- return 68
- short 18
- static 101
- switch 48
- this 137
- true 44
- try 76
- void 99
- while 52

L

Label component, JLabel 138
Lambda expression 126
Layout managers 146
Left shift bitwise operator, << 40
Length property, length 64
Less than operator, < 30
Less than or equal operator, <= 30

Linux operating system 15, 170
List components, JList JComboBox 142
Literals 38
Loading resources 137
LocalDateTime class. *See* Classes
Logical operators
  &&, ||, ! 32
Long data type, long 18
Loop structure
  array elements 70, 72
  break statement 56
  do while loop 54
  for loop 50
  labels 58
  while loop 52
Lottery program 87
Lotto program 168

M

MainActivity.java file 176
Main method 13, 66
Meta file, MANIFEST.MF 172
Methods
  Creating methods 98
  Overloading methods 99
Minimum API level 175
Modulus operator, % 26
Mouse events 160
Multi-dimensional arrays 74
Multiplication operator, * 26

N

Naming conventions 16
Nested statements 46
New keyword, new 64, 108
Newline character 38
NOT bitwise operator, ~ 40
NOT operator, ! 32
Null keyword, null 88

O

Object Oriented Programming (OOP)
  Constructor initialization 112
  Creating an object 106
  Encapsulating properties 110
  Producing an instance 108
OpenJDK 9
Operator precedence 36
Oracle JDK 9
OR bitwise operator, | 40
OR operator, || 32, 45
Overloading methods 99

P

Packages
  java.awt
    Color 148
    Font 148
  java.awt.event
    ActionListener 152, 154
    ItemListener 152, 156
    KeyListener 152, 158
    MouseListener 152, 160
    MouseMotionListener 152, 160
  java.io
    BufferedReader class 118
    BufferedWriter class 122
    File class 116
    FileReader class 120
    FileWriter class 122
    InputStreamReader class 118
  java.lang
    Math class 82, 84, 86
    String class 88, 90, 92, 94
  java.net
    URL 137
  java.text
    NumberFormat class 130
  java.time
    LocalDateTime 128
  java.time.format
    DateTimeFormatter 130
  java.util
    Arrays class 124
  javax.swing
    ButtonGroup 144
    ClassLoader 137

FlowLayout 134
ImageIcon 136
JButton 136
JCheckBox 142
JComboBox 142
JFrame 134
JLabel 138
JList 142
JOptionPane 162, 164
JPanel 134
JRadioButton 144
JScrollPane 140
JTextArea 140
JTextField 140
Palette of controls 177
Passing argument values 99
Passing command line arguments 66, 68
PATH 10
Precedence operator, () 36, 45
Private keyword, private 110
Project window 176
Public keyword, public 102
Push-button component, JButton 136, 154

R

Radio button component, JRadioButton 144
Reading console input 118
Reading files 120
Release version 184
Return keyword, return 68
Right shift bitwise operator, >> 40

S

Scope 100
Short data type, short 18
Signing apps 184
Sorting array elements 124
Statements 44
Static keyword, static 101
String class. *See* Classes
String data type, String 16, 18
String Resources 179
Sub class 104
Subtraction operator, - 26
Sun Microsystems 8
Super class 104
Swing components 134
Switch keyword, switch 48
System class. *See* Classes

T

Terminal window 11
Ternary operator, ? : 34
Testing Android apps 182
Text field components, JTextField JTextArea 140
Text view 177
This keyword, this
  getClass() method 137
Time 128
  Formatter 130
Troubleshooting errors 22
True keyword, true 44
Try keyword, try 76

V

Variable array declaration 64
Variable declaration 16
Version number 11
Void keyword, void 99

W

While keyword, while 52
Window, GUI 134
Writing files 122

X

XOR bitwise operator, ^ 40

Z

ZIP compression format 171, 174